THE NERVE CENTER

NUMBER NINETEEN:
A Joseph V. Hughes, Jr., and Holly O. Hughes
Book in The Presidency and Leadership Series

THE NERVE CENTER

*Lessons in Governing
from the White House
Chiefs of Staff*

Edited by Terry Sullivan

Foreword by James A. Baker, III

TEXAS A&M UNIVERSITY PRESS ✺ COLLEGE STATION

The paper used in this book meets the minimum requirements
of the American National Standard for Permanence
of Paper for Printed Library Materials, z39.48-1984.
Binding materials have been chosen for durability.

Library of Congress Cataloging-in-Publication Data

The nerve center : lessons in governing from the White House chiefs of staff /
edited by Terry Sullivan ; foreword by James A. Baker, III.—1st ed.

p. cm.—(The presidency and leadership ; no. 19)

Includes index.

ISBN 1-58544-349-2 (cloth : alk. paper)

1. Presidents—United States—Staff.   2. United States. White House
Office—Officials and employees.   3. United States—Politics and government—
1945–1989.   4. United States—Politics and government—1989–
I. Sullivan, Terry (Terry O.)   II. Series.

JK552.N47   2004

352.23'72293'0973—dc22   2004001036

So much of what you do in a White House is shaped and affected by what's gone before. There are valuable lessons to be learned in the experiences of earlier administrations that you may want to apply, when faced with similar sets of circumstances.

—Richard Cheney, former White House chief of staff
and vice president of the United States

Contents

Acknowledgments

At the beginning of the presidential election cycle in 1997, everyone knew White House organization would shortly become a center of attention. In three years hence, a new president would move into the White House with new organizational ideas, new policy goals, and, inevitably, a new and untried White House staff. While no one knew then who would lead the new team as chief of staff, many knew firsthand the nature of the challenges he or she would face. And everyone knew how seriously afoul previous administrations had run the ship of state simply because they did not know ahead of time the elementary lessons that working in the White House would eventually teach them.

Three years later, in June, 2000, former Secretary of State James A. Baker, III, stepped into a circle of presidency scholars and reporters and triumphantly declared, "This has been great!" Each in that circle appreciated the significance of his words. He was extolling the just-completed Washington Forum on the Role of the White House Chief of Staff, which had convened an unprecedented collection of leaders—former members of Congress, past Senate and House leaders, past cabinet secretaries, future cabinet secretaries, and, it turned out, at least one future vice president of the United States—who, together with a preeminent group of moderators, spent the day sifting through their experiences as former White House chiefs of staff, trying to clarify the job for a predecessor as yet unnamed.

Putting his hand on my shoulder Secretary Baker proclaimed, "It was Terry's idea." And then after a mischievous pause, he said, " . . . but *I* herded these cats *together*!" Indeed. Late in 1999, Secretary Baker approved a recommendation that the Baker Institute of Rice University put together a conference in Washington designed to simultaneously bolster the institutional memory of the White House and publicly commit the prestige of his colleagues to the idea that presidential candidates needed to plan early. No other group of practitioners had ever made such a bold commitment. Past presidential candidates generally had taken very seriously the possibility that planning to win would generate a public backlash and had regarded such planning as presumptuous. Given his own extensive experience in both national electoral politics and in running government day in and day out, Secretary Baker knew the atmosphere on this issue needed changing. Once personally committed to the proposition, Secretary Baker began to convince his colleagues of its importance and the necessity for their participation. Initially, he convinced two former chiefs of staff, Donald Rumsfeld and Leon E. Panetta, to join him. And with their acceptance, the remaining chiefs of staff quickly followed suit. In the end, only three of the living former chiefs of staff were willing but unable to participate in the forum.

While Secretary Baker herded cats, the Baker Institute began to design the forum. With the assistance of the Woodrow Wilson International Center for Scholars of the Smithsonian Institution and the White House 2001 Project, a nonpartisan consortium of universities and scholars, the Institute prepared a master plan for format and substance. The Wilson Center staff proved immensely valuable to putting on the Forum, tirelessly providing assistance and guidance as well as simply solving logistical problems specific to Washington. Those who worked so diligently there included: Susan Nugent, who coordinated the Forum for the Wilson Center, John Tyler, Michael Van Deusen, Michael Lacey, and Cynthia Ely.

The Institute also received the generous guidance of the White House 2001 Project's director, Martha Joynt Kumar. Her program provided useful background interviews with many of those who have worked in the White House Office of the Chief of Staff, including some of those attending the Forum. In addition, Kenneth Simendinger of the White House 2001 Project staff provided valuable assistance.

At the Baker Institute, everyone pitched in: Hermane Pflieger, Laura Shapiro, Brooke Robertson, Professor Richard Stoll. W. O. King, and Jay Guererro managed all of the logistical elements. We also benefited from the cooperation of the staff at Baker Botts L.L.P., Washington, D.C., and, in particular, Bridgette Montange. In the Houston offices of Baker Botts, Charlotte Border lent a helping hand. After the Forum ended, Robbie Devries of the Baker Institute's Round Table contributed a great deal of her time to oversee editorial changes to the draft transcript. Lora Manning and Sharon Farrett also worked on the transcript by editing changes.

Funding for the Forum came from the generous support of Nancy Jo Allen, a member of the Baker Institute's Round Table.

Without all of the efforts of all of these people, the Forum would not have succeeded in providing this useful record.

Among those who have benefited from the judgment of the Forum, many have helped me develop a record of their 2001 presidential transition, the very focus of the Forum's work. Most notably, these include Secretary Andrew Card, the White House chief of staff for George W. Bush, and Karl Rove, senior counselor to President George W. Bush, who directed the development of the 180-day plan for the transition and has participated as a critical figure (along with Secretary Card) in the long-term planning group of the Bush White House. I acknowledge their own personal involvement, contributing their time discussing with me the transition. And I acknowledge the assistance of Melissa Bennett of Secretary Card's staff and Sue Ralston of Mr. Rove's staff, who individually made possible the time Secretary Card and Mr. Rove committed to helping this project.

Then there are those "cats" Secretary Baker holds in such high esteem—his colleagues as former White House chiefs of staff. This volume constitutes the record of their judgments about this special job. Without their cooperation, of course, none of its text would inform the future. No one but Secretary Baker expected such a passionate commitment by these extraordinarily busy public leaders. Yet every one of them leapt at the opportunity to participate. In a very special way, then, my final acknowledgment must go to those people who, for a period of time, have held this unique responsibility to magnify the time, reach, and voice of the president of the United States.

—Terry Sullivan

Governing from the White House

A Foreword by James A. Baker, III

We created the Baker Institute to organize efforts just like the Forum on the Role of the White House Chief of Staff, bringing scholars and journalists into a dialogue with those who have carried the burdens of office, in this case governing from the White House. It was an extraordinary gathering. I doubt that there have ever been this many former chiefs of staff in the same place at the same time. They are all very busy individuals, and they participated in this Forum at some sacrifice to their personal and professional lives.

THE WORST JOB IN WASHINGTON

My distinguished colleagues and I came to this office from different backgrounds—from Congress and business, from law, and from politics. We all have different policy perspectives. Some of us have even run campaigns to throw others of us out of office.

Despite our varied backgrounds and political views, all of us share one common experience, and that is the experience of holding what I would characterize as the second-toughest job in Washington. When you realize that even though the White House chief of staff has tremendous power, he or she, nevertheless, is not a principal but only a staffer—face it, it's right there in the title— then it is easy to understand why some people also characterize it not just as the second-toughest job in Washington but as the *worst* job in Washington. As the only person in history who was dumb enough to have taken the job twice in his life, I confess that I was sometimes inclined to agree with that characterization.

DISTINCTLY CRITICAL

However you characterize the job, it remains a distinctly critical job to the president, to the executive branch, to the country, and today, given our preeminence, to the world at large. Shortly after an election, somebody wakes up one morning to realize that in a very, very few weeks he or she will lead a team that is not yet picked into America's nerve center.

There's an old saying that every time history repeats itself, the price goes up. It's an aphorism that could have been written with the White House staff in mind. Today, as we all know, White House mistakes reverberate loud and long and, thanks to the revolution in modern communications, at the speed of light.

In short, the challenges facing the White House chief of staff are truly immense and the cost of failure is commensurately high. That's one reason we convened these former White House chiefs of staff and the central reason they came—to lend our collective experiences to whatever administration, Democrat or Republican, assumed office. Unlike much of the political world, where winning and losing matter a great deal and justify strenuous and partisan efforts, good governance knows no party. Managing America's business with grace and ease yields no partisan advantages. It is simply good for America. In realization of that fact, we have all participated to the fullest and have gladly offered our experiences without reservation.

THE MEETING OF FOUR FORCES

When I look back upon my years as White House chief of staff, it strikes me that the job for all of its complexity can pretty much be summed up by four "P"s: people, politics, process, and policy. It is the task of the chief of staff to assist the president in getting the first three of these "P"s right, because you can't get the fourth one without the first three. Only if the president succeeds at managing to govern can the administration fulfill its ultimate goal—the formulation and implementation of effective policy.

PEOPLE

Let me take the first three "P"s one by one, sharing my thoughts on them as a way to foreshadow the Forum's deliberations. I'll begin with people. Now, an administration's choice of key personnel outside the White House, particularly at the very senior and certainly at the cabinet level, is something that usually falls well outside the purview of the chief of staff, but it is incumbent upon the chief of staff to build professional working relationships with senior policy makers based on common goals and on mutual trust. This begins, of course, with the president himself.

The two presidents that I was fortunate to serve, Ronald Reagan and George H. W. Bush, were very different men by way of background and by way of temperament. One I did not know well when I started out as his chief of staff, while the other was an old friend of many years.* Yet I feel that I enjoyed equally good working relationships with both of them. Those relationships, in turn, were grounded in mutual trust and confidence.

Critical to building and maintaining that trust, not just with the president, but with other senior administration personnel, is always remembering that the chief of staff, while very, very powerful, is what the title implies: staff. You can influence where the president goes, you can influence what he does, whom he sees, what he reads, but you are not endowed with any of the legal or constitutional responsibilities for making decisions. This means that, among other things, the chief of staff should not be heard or seen too much. He or she can, and indeed I would argue absolutely should, spend a lot of time with the press so that the administration's view of things gets out. That time should be spent on background.

Another important task involving people is, of course, identifying and recruiting the White House team. Given the painfully brief period that a new administration has to prepare for assuming office, finding the right people with the right talents committed to the administration's goals, prepared to work as a team, and ready to hit the ground running is as absolutely vital as it is extraordinarily difficult.

PROCESS

Making the trains run on time is one accepted definition of the second "P," process. The presidency as a whole, and not just the White House, has to function effectively to concentrate attention on the president's priorities and then, once a decision has been taken, to see to it that that decision is implemented.

For the White House chief of staff, this task primarily means learning to say "no." Ninety-eight percent of the job, I think, or at least I sometimes used to think, is saying "no." There are literally hundreds, if not thousands, of claimants on the president's time, and somebody has to say "not now." That someone is almost always the chief of staff. So it's no wonder that chiefs of staff sometimes feel as if they walk around with targets on both their fronts and their backs.

Running an efficient White House for the president is only one part of the chief of staff's responsibilities. Managing that process also means that the chief of staff has to ensure that the president hears all sides of an issue. While it sounds easy in principle, in practice securing balanced advice is terribly difficult. It's hard for three reasons. First, an effective process is one that must work from the ground up and not just as a last-minute check at the very top. It requires sacrifices from everyone in the White House in order to assure that the president is well served. It's hard, too, because issues often come to the White House at great speed, driven by breaking news. Your process must avoid surprises; it must keep the president from being locked into a bargain in which he has no voice; and it must retain the president's initiative in shaping the national agenda. And it means from time to time, you must raise issues that the president, for whatever reason, might rather avoid. In the Reagan administration, we used to joke about this problem from time to time by saying that President Reagan didn't like "yes men." When he said "no," we all said "no."

POLITICS

A critical component for any chief of staff is the third "P," politics. I'm talking here about politics beyond merely a campaign or electoral sense. In a democracy, politics and policy cannot be separated. There is, in fact, some political component in almost every presidential decision. It either depends upon or impacts upon public opinion. It strengthens or undermines relations with the Congress. And it either underscores or rends asunder the political balance within the administration itself.

Every administration is elected on the basis of a coalition of voters, and every administration contains individuals with a variety of ideological convictions. President Reagan used to say frequently that our right hand never knew what our *far* right hand was doing. That joke, as most of his jokes did, held an important kernel of truth: politics extends to within an administration itself.

Because the chief of staff stands uniquely at the intersection of politics and policy, he or she should be the president's chief political advisor. It's the chief of staff's job to spell out the political meaning of a decision while also having a full grasp and understanding of its policy implications. In my own case, I found that experience in electoral campaigns was an immense help in serving the president and in serving his policy agenda.

POLICY

Finally, it is that fourth "P," the president's policy agenda, that really counts. It is the prize on which every chief of staff must concentrate. While focus begins with the transition, the president's policy focus must continue long after the thrill of electoral victory has gone. It's very easy, in fact all too easy, for a new administration's policy agenda to drift off course. Assuring that it does not is the chief of staff's ultimate responsibility. In the face of external criticism, internal conflict, and just sheer fatigue, the chief of staff has to find ways to reinvigorate, even reinvent, the policy process in a manner that advances the president's agenda.

---

* Mr. Baker joined the Reagan campaign in 1980 when then-candidate Reagan's campaign merged with the campaign team of George H. W. Bush, Reagan's chief opponent in the Republican primaries and then picked as Reagan's running mate. Mr. Baker had known Mr. Bush for a number of years and had directed Mr. Bush's presidential campaign. Mr. Baker initially served as head of the briefing team preparing Mr. Reagan for the presidential debates with President Jimmy Carter. After considering others for the post, including his campaign manager, Mr. Edmund Meese III, candidate Reagan asked Mr. Baker if he would serve as chief of staff in the new administration.—Editor

THE NERVE CENTER

Two Operational Dilemmas

An Introduction by Terry Sullivan

*I started out in effect not having [a] Chief of Staff and it didn't work.
So, anybody who doesn't have one and tries to run the responsibilities
of the White House, I think, is putting too big a burden on the
President himself. You need a filter, a person that you have total
confidence in who works so closely with you that in effect his is almost
an alter ego. I just can't imagine a President not having an effective
Chief of Staff.*

—*Gerald R. Ford, White House 2001 Project*

The American White House sits at the nerve center of world history. Its policies reach into every part of the American experience. Its bustling daily routines become the subject of serious conversations the world over. At the core
of this nerve center, a bureaucratic operation extends the reach and magnifies
the voice of the American president. The White House chief of staff manages
that operation. So important has that office become, that to ignore its requirements tempts presidential fate itself. As one of the last to eschew a chief of staff,
President Gerald R. Ford's words on the subject carry a special message: What
we do not know about this office imperils the republic.

The range of what we do not know astonishes. No systematic scholarly literature has ever developed sufficient to answer the critical questions facing a
working White House. No systematic theory has developed, resting on the
kind of articulated central principles now common in the study of all other
American policy institutions. Because of these two gaps, presidency scholars
cannot "talk truth to power" when the subject turns to presidential transitions

and the related topic of governing from the White House. Instead, scholars must rely upon the willingness of power to talk truth to them. The Forum on the White House Chief of Staff represents one of those rare instances when just that happened.

This essay outlines the gaps in knowledge that their discussions tried to fill. It describes these gaps by asserting two operational dilemmas facing a White House: one about discipline and the other about effectiveness. This book will return to these two dilemmas in a final chapter analyzing the George W. Bush presidential transition in 2001, the transition immediately following the Forum, as a part of the governing cycle these chiefs discussed. This introduction also highlights the rhythms of an administration's tenure, from start to restart to reelection and closing out. While this book takes as a principal theme that no one can conduct a presidential transition properly without knowing the nature of governing itself, it also takes seriously the notion that presidential transitions lie on a seamless continuum with governing during the presidential tenure, as well. Each of these portions of a president's tenure presents its own special challenges to those chiefs of staff who stand their watches then. And, echoing the importance of these two dilemmas, each period presents persistent challenges common to every White House chief of staff who accepts the responsibility for the nerve center.

TWO FUNCTIONS OF THE WHITE HOUSE STAFF

The White House staff fills two presidential needs. First, it extends the president's reach. It expands the breadth of presidential "awareness" by gathering intelligence, assessing information, and overseeing policy deliberations. It expands presidential strategic considerations, which makes it possible to consider a wider range of alternative scenarios simultaneously. The staff also expands opportunities for controlling implementation by requiring the executive always to anticipate the president's reaction. In a way, the staff affords the president something akin to the advantages of the Congress, where its multitudes create a policy-making institution that "never sleeps."

Second, the White House staff magnifies the president's voice. It creates a wider range of "presidential presence" by coordinating the administration's "message." And it provides the capacity to elaborate the president's position on issues, thereby increasing the likely force of presidential persuasion in public deliberations. The White House staff ensures that the president has the most forceful voice in public debate.

THE NERVE CENTER

The president's staff works in an extraordinary place. At one point during the Forum, former Carter chief of staff Jack Watson told the audience that the skills a chief of staff uses to maneuver successfully through that special community involve nothing more than the common decency everyone learns from their parents. In effect, simply getting along dominates White House operations. Maybe so. That comment notwithstanding, everyone attending the Forum acknowledged that White House work differs from work elsewhere.

Often, a critical mistake for a new staff is the way in which they project previous experience—in state government, business, or in Congress—onto their new White House responsibilities. They understand the White House as something different, but only by degrees. They talk about their past experience as having prepared them because they have experienced "the big leagues." In fact, they come to learn that thinking in terms of the human nervous system would constitute a better analogy than this very popular baseball one. The human nerve center does not merely equal the sum of its appended parts; it does not differ only by degrees. As a consequence, understanding the senses does not lay a substantial foundation for understanding the brain. Instead, the nerve center differs in nature from the sum of its reporting subsystems. In this same way, the White House is different from other organizations. It differs in scale, surely, but it differs in other ways as well: in scrutiny and in partisanship, from anything anyone has previously experienced.

Scale

White House operations have a distinctive "scale." For one thing, they outpace work elsewhere. Operations accelerate as they approach the American government's center. At the Forum, former Clinton chief of staff and private financier Erskine Bowles described the work pace as "faster than a dot-com." Clay Johnson III, himself a former executive for PepsiCo and a onetime director of presidential personnel for President Bush, described the White House pace in similar terms. "At PepsiCo," he recalled, "we had some times that were as fast-paced, whenever we were about to launch a new product we had invested a billion dollars in and whose outcome would either send our stock skyrocketing or crash-land it. The difference was that at PepsiCo, that pace might last for a week once a year. At the White House, it is every day, Saturday and Sunday, too!"[1]

In addition, as operations move to the center, they multiply demands. In personnel, for example, the governor of a large state must find nominees for hundreds of state positions. To fill these positions, the governor's staff must wade through a pool of potential applicants, ranging in the thousands but usually not more than 15,000.[2] A presidential administration must fill slightly less than 8,200 positions. To fill those positions, the White House might maintain applications from hundreds of thousands of potential nominees. The Clinton database, for example, maintained 195,000 dossiers. A president-elect easily might receive 10,000 applications on the single day following election. Indeed, everything having to do with White House operations carries such an exclamation point. Without adequate preparations, the scale of White House operations can simply overwhelm a president's staff.

The more challenging aspect of scale, though, derives not from sheer size but instead from the juxtaposition between what the staff has faced, and has some sense of, and what it now faces, and has no sense of. In personnel, again as an example, the fact of scale, daunting enough on its own, means that the initial strategy for handling applications can easily capsize White House operations. In turn, a foundering personnel operation can lead to a range of embarrassing and failed appointments. These in their turn undermine the president's reputation for competence so critical to success in the complicated Washington policy-making community. So, a misunderstanding of the simple scale of presidential appointments quickly escalates into a reputational catastrophe for the president affecting not only the transition but the rest of the administration's future.

Scrutiny

Simply put, the nerve center commands a worldwide audience. One former staff member described this scrutiny as if "you were naked in a glass house every minute."[3] This intense scrutiny lends special weight to the words and actions of those responsible to the chief of staff. Because the White House constitutes one pole of almost every news story, those words and actions are under twenty-four-hour surveillance. Scrutiny also makes it impossible for a chief of staff to remain a detached and shadowy figure in an administration. Moreover, since every misstep draws instant attention and since the pace of operations spins wildly, each misdirection diverts the administration's energies by unleashing often uncontrollable forces that not only complicate work but send secondary responses rippling through the policy-making apparatus. Scrutiny amplifies political stakes and places a premium on flawless eloquence. Misstatements tolerated in a national campaign or the state house suddenly wreck diplomatic initiatives and sap political allies of their legitimacy when made at the White House.

Partisanship

Despite the declining importance of party in determining who governs, partisanship has become the defining atmospheric of governing. From the convoluted web of ethical standards, to the easily escalating tensions in congressional deliberations, to the omnipresent threat of subpoena, White House work has taken on an extraordinarily partisan dimension. Governing in this new Washington environment places special strains on any chief of staff's operation. For example, the omnipresence of escalating crises complicates the distribution of responsibilities. The constantly growing target on their backs undermines any chief of staff's chances of remaining in office long enough to apply hard-learned lessons. And the tension inherent in poisonous partisanship skews every "normal" operational element, from staff meetings in which no one keeps notes to the necessity for "edgy" messages in public debate.

TWO OPERATIONAL DILEMMAS

When the nerve center, with its scale, scrutiny, and partisanship, impinges on the White House staff, two results occur. First, it presents the chief of staff with two operational dilemmas, balances to maintain between equally important forces. The first dilemma pits the individual's need for policy influence against the broader need for a disciplined decision-making process. The second dilemma pits the staff's ability to respond to crises against its need to effectively advance the president's agenda.

Second, the nerve center warps time. More than any other institution of American power, time enmeshes the presidency. While members of Congress must regularly stand for reelection and thus feel the rhythm of tenure, the twenty-third constitutional amendment presents every president with time's inescapable limitations. And while the American public believes every administration deserves a successful start, it expects performance within a finite period. Keeping ahead of the changing environment presented by eroding tenure becomes every chief of staff's defining constraint. These two broad categories of effects, operational dilemmas and the passage of tenure, became the organizing tenet for the Forum's discussions.

Initiative vs. Orchestration

As Secretary James Baker pointed out in his foreword, every White House exists at the confluence of four forces: personnel, process, politics, and policy.

Selecting and managing personnel constitutes the starting point for everything else. The person who becomes a president's chief of staff presents an imposing figure when he takes office—nothing at all like the "neutral-competent" bureaucrat yearning for anonymity so often associated with recommendations about White House staffs.[4] Indeed, all the former chiefs of staff have come from successful careers in partisan politics, in business, in policy advocacy, or as fierce campaigners for one candidate against another. In their new positions, though, these previously successful individuals have to subrogate their past successes and experiences to the rigors of holding positions as mere staff, exercising "reflected" powers, and managing a collection of people with these same characteristics facing these same imperatives. Those who performed well in the job could adapt to these circumstances, disciplining their own policy interests in favor of the president's.[5]

In effect, White House operations revolve around a dilemma reflected in this daunting personal challenge for chiefs of staff. An administration draws its energy from the staff of policy advocates who pursue their personal ambitions for making policy through their advocacy and the president's decisions. This ambition to have their views validated in presidential decisions (what better way to underscore their value than to have the president adopt their advice?) brings staff to work and compensates them for their arduous efforts. At the same time, this desire to have their views validated can undermine as well as invigorate. When thwarted by the kind of decision-making process that presents all important sides of an issue to the president, this creative force borne of personal ambition can generate a cold cunning and competition among advisors. Many a White House has benefited by the creative tension generated by such ambitions and many have faltered when those same ambitions turn inward against themselves.

We might characterize this dilemma as pitting initiative against orchestration. Individual ambitions create energy in the White House (initiative) reined in and controlled by a routine of orderly decision making (orchestration). Call this dilemma "discipline," because the balance developed between individual ambition and collective routine requires discipline to maintain.

What hazards must a new chief face in maintaining discipline for the president? Obviously, midcourse chiefs, those brought in to put the administration on a new footing, face this dilemma's most severe variants. President Clinton's second chief of staff, Leon Panetta, alternated between characterizing his situation as "organizing a soccer team among elementary school kids" (everyone racing for the ball!) and as "taking a battlefield promotion" (restructuring business while taking fire). How can they build a team of advocates willing to forego their private motives in order to serve the president's?

A particularly intriguing void in our knowledge of White House operations entails how the habits of presidents affect the resolution of this dilemma. When the president's own tried and true practices run up against the pressures of White House process and pace, what must give way? Does the White House staff reflect the president's strengths or does the staff compensate for weaknesses? How much can a president contribute to or alleviate the chief's trials over discipline?

Reaction vs. Projection

A second operational dilemma involves the confluence of politics and process. As mentioned earlier, an unbelievable pace constitutes one of the defining characteristics of the nerve center. The operational efficiency of the White House staff under this extraordinary pace becomes a common measure of the president's capacity for leadership. Though a third of all chiefs of staff assumed office because a crisis had claimed their predecessor, every chief of staff has faced troubled times when the administration's leadership began to erode. Every deployment of White House staff, then, must accommodate distractions. The ability to do so constitutes a critical element of an administration's success. For example, former chief of staff Dick Cheney noted that "Stuff happens. Lots of times your presidency is more completely defined by how you deal with the stuff that happens than it is by how you deal with the regularly scheduled events that occur during the course of the year. If there's an area where the transitions are inadequate, it's this whole area of managing crises."[6] Maintaining a focus on the president's agenda becomes one of the central challenges of crisis management.[7]

Maintaining a focus in the presence of great distraction, of course, poses an organizational conundrum. If an administration's current operations can accommodate those extraordinary challenges, then the staff system must have worked previously at less than full pace. In effect, the ability to accommodate a crisis perforce implies underutilization of normal capacity for projecting the president's leadership. On the other hand, if they cannot accommodate these challenges, then the president's team faces a hostile world in which they may lose their leadership when a crisis arises. Call this dilemma "effectiveness," for it underscores politics and policy.

Governor Sununu raised this concern at the Forum during his discussion of the transition period, reflecting his and President Bush's choice in favor of slack resources. His discussion of the problem clearly indicated the central role the president's judgment on this matter and his expectations played in setting the pace of White House staff work. How do chiefs of staff build a staff operation capable of handling crisis but fully utilizing their talents in normal operational times?

In addition, maintaining a focus on the president's agenda involves projecting that agenda, especially into the future. Just as the meaning of every candidate lies not in what they presently do but what they intend to do, the meaning of every presidency from the moment of its transition lies in its future. But to carry out this planning for the future, again, presents the White House staff with a dilemma: planning inherently means sacrificing capacity in the here and now in favor of projecting success into a future that may never come. This planning variant on effectiveness can confound any administration. Ambitious White House staff do not want to find themselves assigned to long-term planning groups fearing that to do so sacrifices daily operational involvement. They fear that those who master the here and now will always get to carry out any future plans, even those devised by others. So for aides, the demands of the here and now always trump the potential for the future and always draw their attention. How can the chief of staff get aides to sacrifice their involvement in daily operations in order to establish the precursors for later decision making?

THE RHYTHMS OF PRESIDENTIAL TENURE

While the patterns of operations remain constant, the rhythms of White House work vary over time. For example, all of the pressures that result from the nerve center—its pace, scrutiny, and partisanship—vary little as time passes. On the other hand, the administration's capacity to deal with these pressures fluctuates as the White House team "ages" in office and then cycles out the door.

Nowhere does a chief of staff have more control over the job than during the presidential transition and the initial weeks of the new administration. Thus, the first Forum discussion, "Starting the White House," directly addresses the interplay of operations with the rhythms of tenure. It focused on defining an effective White House from its starting point in the presidential transition.

Planning for winning presents a host of troublesome contradictions for operations. Each presidential candidate knows that the transition offers a limited window of opportunity that requires detailed plans to master. Yet candidates typically eschew the early planning necessary for mastery. They worry that planning to win distracts the campaign from winning. They worry that the public will see making plans to govern as presumptuous, yielding a distraction from the campaign's main themes. And they often have unbridled confidence in their ability to master the challenges of governing from the

White House. After all, they have mastered what they have faced heretofore. For many reasons, candidates often cannot get beyond the fear that no matter how low-keyed they keep it, early planning will derail their campaign. Yet few recommendations garner more universal appreciation than the former chiefs of staff's suggestion that transition planning must begin well before election day.

Planning for personnel issues poses a second set of challenges. For that reason, most of the chiefs of staff agreed that a substantial amount of the early planning effort should focus on personnel, both in terms of identifying critical positions and in creating a decision-making process. In that process, some observers and practitioners maintain that presidents-elect must prepare to distance themselves from loyal campaigners, favoring instead those "wiser Washington hands" that can contribute their experience in the governing community. Plenty of presidential transitions, the record shows, have stumbled through problems of their own making, easily avoided had they had wiser hands on the controls.

Others counter that Washington hands too easily give up on the president's agenda, bending to the "realities" of governing in Washington. Campaign hands, on the other hand, "know the president," remember why they had gotten to the White House, and prefer to keep faith with that agenda. Clearly, then, this balance between campaigning and governing must trouble every chief of staff when starting a White House. What are the choices that present themselves in finding a balance? How can a chief of staff resolve this challenge?

The second Forum discussion followed the administration through what Bill Plante called "a slight bump in the road or perhaps a train wreck." In it, the former chiefs of staff discussed the stresses of coming to a White House under fire. Crisis management surely differs from normal management, even in the White House, where crises arrive at the doorstep with the morning's news summary. What critical reins of power did these chiefs of staff need to grasp to reverse the situation? What kinds of assurances did they seek from the president? Must a new chief of staff control Oval Office access? Must a new chief of staff "clean house," replacing the previous staff with a new group?

From reelection to legacy, the third Forum discussion focused on the last act in White House tenure. How clearly can one delineate the responsibilities for governing and the demands of reelection? How clearly can the White House draw a distinction between its responsibilities to the country and its commitments to the party for successfully achieving reelection? What kinds of decisions or initiatives does the White House put on hold during a campaign? How can a chief of staff control the pressures for executive orders, regulatory actions, and pardons?

IN THE WASHINGTON COMMUNITY

The White House sits at the center of a great constitutional contrivance inside a city of that contrivance. The Forum's last discussion concerned bridging the constitutional gap between Congress and the executive branch. This last discussion reflected more than a simple concern with Washington context. The former chiefs of staff covered an additional issue: how to plan for the anticipated constitutional change coming? The presidential election season of 2000 presented the nation with a clear opportunity to manage change; President Clinton's tenure had become fully enshrouded in the constitutional requirements for succession. As Secretary Baker mentioned in his foreword, a morning would shortly arrive when someone yet unknown would awake to the awesome responsibility of building a new administration from the ground up. That Andrew Card, whom all of them knew and with whom most of them had served, would bear that responsibility for George W. Bush and Forum participant Dick Cheney did not minimize the challenge before the former chiefs of staff to reshape perspectives on transition planning. The Forum of former chiefs of staff set out to underscore that the country could not afford to forego this historic opportunity and to reiterate the Washington community's expectations that transition planning should constitute the normal course of campaign business.

Built on momentum created by the Forum on the Role of the White House Chief of Staff and maintained by the coordinated efforts of the Baker Institute and other public interest groups, transition planning became a reality. Both of the major party campaigns quietly established planning groups, built up potential personnel rosters, and identified critical organizational decisions for their candidate's consideration once elected. All of these plans and the momentum for planning played an important role in effecting a productive transition after the events of election day 2000 and decision day, December 12. Without the message delivered by this group in that moment, a murky future could easily have unfolded from the Florida decision. Instead, as the last chapter will detail, the 2001 transition proceeded to set records for discipline and effectiveness, mastering personnel and process while merging politics to accomplish policy.

Notes

1. Clay Johnson III, conversation with Terry Sullivan, May 5, 2001, Cambridge, Mass.
2. Texas, for example, typically maintains a database of 15,000 resumes.
3. "Interview with Alonzo MacDonald," White House 2001 Project, White House Interview Program, Martha J. Kumar, Feb. 15, 2000, Washington, D.C. See also similar comments by President Ford's director of presidential

personnel, Douglas Bennett, "Interview with Douglas Bennett," White House 2001 Project, White House Interview Program, Martha J. Kumar, Nov. 15, 1999, Washington, D.C.

4. President's Committee on Administrative Management, *Report of the Committee* (Washington, D.C.: Government Printing Office, 1937). In their report, the committee described the central assets of those who would serve the president: "They should be men in whom the President has personal confidence and whose character and attitude is such that they would not attempt to exercise power on their own account. They should be possessed of high competence, great physical vigor, and a *passion for anonymity* [emphasis added]."

5. Lloyd Cutler characterized the White House as similar to the Democratic party: "[It] resembles a city hall. It is very, very difficult to organize. It isn't as if General Electric bought a company and sent in a management team that had worked together for twenty years and then they came to reshape this company that they bought." See "Interview with Lloyd Cutler," White House 2001 Project, White House Interview Program, July 8, 1999, Martha J. Kumar, Washington, D.C.

6. "Interview with Richard Cheney," White House 2001 Project, White House Interview Program, Martha J. Kumar, July 29, 1999, Dallas, Texas.

7. The seventeen who have held the office in the modern presidency compose three distinct groups: those starting an administration (transition), those who took over in a crisis (redirection), and those who inherited the relative calm after the righted ship (routine). Since James A. Baker, III, held the office twice, seventeen individuals have occupied eighteen regimes.

CHAPTER I

Members of the Forum

The Forum represented the largest gathering of former White House chiefs of staff since the inception of the office in the post–World War II era. They came together for one extraordinary day to accomplish two goals: First, they wanted to publicly share their thoughts on governing from the White House and to demonstrate that regardless of partisan differences, the experience presented a number of lessons common to them all. "Some of us tried to run others of us out of office," said former Secretary of State James A. Baker, III, "but we all have similar lessons to convey and we all cherish this office for its importance to the presidency." Second, the former chiefs of staff wanted to lend their personal support to the notion that major presidential candidates needed to plan early for the presidential transition and that the public should see this planning as responsible.

The Forum consisted of four discussions, each including some subset of former chiefs of staff and each coordinated by a convener. The latter included a former member of Congress, two journalists, and a respected presidential scholar.

BIOGRAPHIES OF PARTICIPANTS

Howard H. Baker, Jr., served President Ronald W. Reagan as White House chief of staff from February, 1987, until July, 1988. He is a native of Tennessee. Currently, Senator Baker is U.S. ambassador to Japan. He is also a partner in the Washington law firm of Baker, Donelson, Bearman and Caldwell. In 1966, Senator Baker became the first Republican ever popularly elected to the U.S. Senate from Tennessee, and he won reelection by wide margins in 1972 and

1978. He concluded his Senate career by serving two terms as Minority Leader (1977–81) and two terms as Majority Leader (1981–85), which Senator Baker called the "best job in Washington." Senator Baker serves on the Board of Directors of Pennzoil–Quaker State Company. He serves as a member of the Smithsonian Board of Regents, and he is the chairman of Cherokee Aviation.

James A. Baker, III, served longer and more presidents as the White House chief of staff than any other living individual. He served President Ronald W. Reagan as chief of staff from 1981 to 1985 and President George H. W. Bush in 1992. He is a native Texan. Long active in American presidential politics, Mr. Baker led presidential campaigns for Presidents Ford, Reagan, and Bush over the course of five consecutive presidential elections from 1976 to 1992. After leaving the White House, Mr. Baker served as the sixty-seventh secretary of the treasury from 1985 to 1988 under President Reagan. Mr. Baker also served as the nation's sixty-first secretary of state from January, 1989, through August, 1992, under President Bush. During his tenure at the State Department, Mr. Baker traveled to ninety foreign countries as the United States confronted the unprecedented challenges and opportunities of the post–Cold War era, including the Desert Storm conflict. Mr. Baker is presently a senior partner in the law firm of Baker Botts and senior counselor to the Carlyle Group, a merchant banking firm in Washington, D.C. Mr. Baker is honorary chairman of the James A. Baker III Institute for Public Policy of Rice University. He also serves on the boards of Rice University and the Howard Hughes Medical Institute.

Erskine Bowles served President William J. Clinton as White House chief of staff from November, 1996, until November, 1998. Mr. Bowles was assistant to the president and deputy chief of staff from October, 1994, through December, 1995. He is a native of North Carolina. Currently, Mr. Bowles is a general partner with both Forstmann Little, a major New York private equity firm, and Carousel Capital, the Charlotte-based merchant bank that he co-founded in 1996. Mr. Bowles also serves as chairman of Intelisys Electronic Commerce, a business-to-business e-commerce company. Mr. Bowles now serves as vice chairman of Carolinas HealthCare Authority. He also previously served as president of the Juvenile Diabetes Foundation. Before serving in the White House, Mr. Bowles was administrator of the U.S. Small Business Administration from May, 1993, through September, 1994.

Richard Cheney served President Gerald R. Ford as White House chief of staff from November, 1975, through January, 1977. Mr. Cheney is a native of Wyoming. He has served five terms as a member of the U.S. House of Representatives from Wyoming and was elected House Minority Whip by members of the Republican Conference. Mr. Cheney resigned from the Congress to serve President George H. W. Bush as secretary of defense from March, 1989, through January, 1993, managing America's involvement in Desert Storm. He received the Presidential Medal of Freedom in 1991. After leaving government, Mr. Cheney served as a senior fellow at the American Enterprise Institute and then as CEO and chairman of Halliburton Company, a Dallas-based service company in the oil business. He currently serves with President George W. Bush as the vice president of the United States.

Edward P. Djerejian served President William J. Clinton as U.S. ambassador to Israel. Previously, he served both Presidents Bush and Clinton as assistant secretary of state for Near Eastern Affairs (1991–93) and Presidents Reagan and Bush as U.S. ambassador to the Syrian Arab Republic (1988–91). He is a native New Yorker. Currently, he is director of the James A. Baker III Institute for Public Policy of Rice University. He served President Reagan as special assistant and deputy press secretary for foreign affairs. Mr. Djerejian received the Presidential Distinguished Service Award from President Clinton in 1994, the Department of State's Distinguished Honor Award in 1993, and numerous other honors, including the President's Meritorious Service Award in 1988, the Ellis Island Medal of Honor in 1993, and the Anti-Defamation League's Moral Statesman Award in 1994.

Kenneth M. Duberstein served President Ronald W. Reagan as White House chief of staff from July, 1988, to the conclusion of the administration in 1989. He is a native of Brooklyn. Currently, Mr. Duberstein is chairman and CEO of the Duberstein Group providing strategic planning and consulting services. His earlier government service included stints in the Reagan White House as assistant to the president for legislative affairs and as deputy chief of staff. He also served in the Ford administration's Department of Labor as deputy under secretary and at the General Services Administration as director of congressional relations. He has served the Congress as assistant to Senator Jacob Javits of New York. Mr. Duberstein sits on the board of the Boeing Company, Fannie Mae, and the American Stock Exchange, among others.

Lee H. Hamilton served for thirty-four years as a member of the U.S. House of Representatives from Indiana. As a consequence, he has been on the Washington scene through the tenure of almost all of the former chiefs of staff participating in the Forum. Currently, Mr. Hamilton serves as the director of the Woodrow Wilson International Center for Scholars, the Forum's host. As a member of Congress, Mr. Hamilton served on the Committee of Foreign Affairs as chair of its subcommittee on the Middle East and Europe for more than thirty years. He chaired several select committees, including the Select Committee on Intelligence and the Select Committee to Investigate Covert Arms Transactions with Iran.

Marvin Kalb served as a chief diplomatic correspondent for CBS News and NBC News, and as moderator of *Meet the Press.* He recently retired as the executive director of the Washington office of the Joan Shorenstein Center on the Press, Politics and Public Policy of Harvard University's John Kennedy School of Government. He is a native New Yorker. Currently, he co-directs the Shorenstein's "Vanishing Voter" research project. He also hosted the PBS series *Candidates '88,* and he has appeared regularly on PBS's *Newshour* and many other radio and television programs. Mr. Kalb received numerous awards for excellence in diplomatic reporting. The author of nine books, including two best-selling novels, Mr. Kalb is now writing a book about Washington journalism in the midst of scandal.

Thomas F. "Mack" McLarty served President William J. Clinton as White House chief of staff from January, 1993, until mid-1994. Mr. McLarty remained in service to President Clinton until July, 1998, taking several posts in the White House. A native of Arkansas, Mr. McLarty has an accomplished career in business as chairman and CEO of Fortune 500 companies, served in his state legislature, and chaired the Arkansas State Democratic Party. His Arkla Corporation grew into one of the nation's largest natural gas distributors. Currently, he is vice chairman of Kissinger McLarty Associates, a consulting firm providing strategic services to multinational businesses. Mr. McLarty serves on the boards of the *Financial Times,* Edelman Public Relations, Entergy, and Axciom, among others.

Richard E. Neustadt served Presidents Harry S. Truman and Dwight D. Eisenhower. He was Douglas Dillon Professor Emeritus at Harvard University's John Kennedy School of Government. Professor Neustadt wrote *Presidential Power,* probably the single most influential book on the American presidency, and coauthor of *Thinking in Time,* among other works. He served as a consultant to Presidents Kennedy and Johnson. Neustadt's most recent book, *Report to JFK: The Skybolt Crisis in Perspective,* deals with one of his consulting assignments.

Leon E. Panetta served President William J. Clinton as the White House chief of staff from July, 1994, until January, 1997. He is a native of California. Currently, Mr. Panetta co-directs, with his wife Sylvia, the Leon and Sylvia Panetta Institute for Public Policy, based at California State University, Monterey Bay, a university he helped establish. Mr. Panetta started public service in 1966 working for the Senate Democratic Whip. In 1969 he served in the Nixon administration as special assistant to the secretary of health, education, and welfare and then director of the U.S. Office for Civil Rights, where he was responsible for enforcement of equal education laws. In 1970, he joined Mayor John Lindsay's administration in New York City. In 1977, he began sixteen years service as a member of the U.S. House of Representatives. He then joined the Clinton administration in 1993 as the director of the Office of Management and Budget. Panetta serves on a number of boards and as distinguished scholar to the chancellor of the California State University system.

Bill Plante has served as a CBS News White House correspondent during several administrations, beginning his most recent stint in January, 1993. He is a native of Chicago. His reports are seen regularly on *CBS Evening News with Dan Rather* and CBS News's *This Morning*. Before coming to the White House, Mr. Plante was CBS News's state department correspondent, where he covered the Gulf War diplomacy; the changing U.S.-Soviet relationship during that period; and the 1991 Middle East peace talks, among others. For seven years, he served as anchor of *CBS Sunday Night News*. He has covered a number of presidential campaigns since joining CBS News in 1964. He served four tours of duty in Vietnam for CBS News and covered the civil rights movement in the United States. His reporting has earned him several awards, including four Emmys.

John D. Podesta served President William J. Clinton as White House chief of staff from November, 1998, through to the close of the administration on January 20, 2001. A native of Chicago, Mr. Podesta currently serves on the faculty of law at the Georgetown University Law Center. Mr. Podesta served President Clinton as his first staff secretary. After a two-year teaching stint at Georgetown University Law Center, Mr. Podesta returned to President Clinton's White House as deputy chief of staff. He has had extensive government experience in both the legislative and executive branches. Mr. Podesta served as chief counsel for the Senate Committee on Agriculture, Nutrition and Forestry. He has served as special assistant to the director of Action, a federal volunteer agency, and served as trial attorney in the Department of Justice, Land and Natural Resources Division. Before joining the Clinton administration, Professor Podesta served as president and general counsel of Podesta Associates, Inc., a Washington, D.C., government relations and public affairs firm.

Donald Rumsfeld served President Gerald R. Ford as White House chief of staff and member of the president's cabinet, 1974–75, leaving that post to become the thirteenth U.S. secretary of defense, 1975–77. He is a native of Illinois. Currently, Mr. Rumsfeld serves President George W. Bush as U.S. secretary of defense. He was past chairman of the Board of Directors of Gilead Sciences, Inc. He recently completed service as chairman of the U.S. Government Commission to Assess the Ballistic Missile Threat to the United States and is currently a member of the U.S. Trade Deficit Review Commission. He served four terms in the U.S. Congress. In 1969, he resigned from Congress to join the president's cabinet. He served as director of the Office of Economic Opportunity and assistant to the president, and later as director of the Economic Stabilization Program and counselor to the president, and as U.S. ambassador to the North Atlantic Treaty Organization.

Samuel K. Skinner served President George H. W. Bush as the White House chief of staff during 1992. He is a native of Chicago. Currently, Mr. Skinner is co-chairman of Hopkins and Sutter, after recently retiring as president of the Commonwealth Edison Company and its holding company, Unicom Corporation, one of the nation's largest electric utilities. Prior to his White House service, Mr. Skinner served in President Bush's cabinet for nearly three years as secretary of transportation. Before joining the cabinet, Mr. Skinner was chairman of Chicago's Regional Transportation Authority. His government service includes being appointed U.S. district attorney by President Gerald Ford.

John H. Sununu served President George H. W. Bush as White House chief of staff from January, 1989, until March, 1992. He is a native of New Hampshire. Currently, Mr. Sununu is president of JHS Associates, Ltd., in Washington, D.C. Mr. Sununu became New Hampshire's seventy-fifth governor on January 6, 1983, and served three consecutive terms. He assumed office with a background of nearly twenty years experience as an educator, engineer, small businessman, and community leader. He served as the 1987 chair of the National Governors' Association. From 1992 until 1998, Governor Sununu cohosted CNN's nightly *Crossfire* program, a news/public affairs discussion program. He a member of the Board of Trustees for the George H. W. Bush Presidential Library Foundation.

Jack H. Watson, Jr., served President Jimmy Carter as White House chief of staff during 1980 through the end of the administration in January, 1981. He is a native Georgian. Currently, Mr. Watson recently retired as chief legal strategist of Monsanto Company, a worldwide life sciences company engaged in developing and marketing agricultural products, pharmaceuticals, and food ingredients. Mr. Watson began his government service as chairman of the board of the Georgia Department of Human Resources from 1972 to 1977, during the governorships of Jimmy Carter and George Busbee. He directed President Carter's transition team. He has been a director of the Franklin D. Roosevelt Presidential Library and the Franklin and Eleanor Roosevelt Institute since 1986. In 1987–88, he chaired the Twentieth Century Fund Task Force on the United States Vice Presidency. He served as a trustee and vice chair of the Milton S. Eisenhower Foundation in Washington, D.C., from 1994 to 1998.

CHAPTER 2

Starting the White House

In the spring of 1999, Governor George W. Bush decided two things. First, he decided to run for president. Second, he decided to begin planning for what to do after he had won. For the latter job, he called on his longtime friend and associate Clay Johnson III. The governor charged Mr. Johnson with learning all that he could about how to create a successful transition. When the opportunity arrived to form a new administration, those plans would serve them well (see "Assessing Transition 2001"). Nothing, however, would prove more valuable than the chance to listen to advice from those who had carried out a transition. The discussion that follows here represents some of that good advice, bringing together former chiefs of staff who have managed the transfer of power and the beginning of a new administration.

An administration's work begins before its election and seamlessly stretches into the future. Of course, shaping a successful transition depends upon understanding the governing to follow. And although a transition's structure changes as White House work progresses, those changes only gradually reduce the influence of the critical choices made early on. Changes in the transition's structure have less to do with the mere passage of time than with the maturing of a governing operation. Therefore, many of the issues touched on in this first discussion recur in each of the discussions to follow.

This first discussion among the former chiefs of staff concentrates on facing a transition. Their talks ranged across a number of topics: what needs doing, how to order priorities, the pressures on selection of personnel, how to organize responsibilities, and how to make the best of early opportunities. No one knows better how to properly combine these tasks into a governing White House.

As Secretary Baker has pointed out, starting a White House depends upon people. Chiefs of staff must combine the decision-making process and the president's chosen personnel into a workable and effective advisory apparatus. A good deal of transition planning, therefore, focuses on personnel issues. Among those academics who have assessed presidential governing, the role of former campaign staffs has remained a mystery. How, they wonder, do administrations properly function while relying so heavily on those attuned to campaigning rather than governing? The scholarly literature has come to focus on this element as one of the critical causal factors for the "permanent campaign" and "polarized politics," the growing use of campaign techniques in governing inappropriate to the nature of constitutional leadership. Yet presidents-elect and presidents in office naturally rely heavily on those with whom they have come through the crucible of an election. How a chief of staff might meld these two groups—those with candidate experience and those with Washington experience—into a functioning whole becomes one of the keystone topics of this first discussion.

Bringing staffs together into a single functioning whole can challenge the ablest administrators. Many chiefs of staff have failed to rein in the centrifugal forces that undermine a well-functioning staff because they have not received the authority necessary for the task. The following discussion considers the nature of that authority and how it affects not only the transition but the remainder of the administration's tenure.

The final major issue of transitions addressed in this discussion does not occur regularly in the other discussions because transitions represent a special period in which the president and the White House staff have an opportunity to establish relationships anew. Even a president with a long Washington resume has an opportunity to change things dramatically with the transition to power. How do chiefs of staff structure these new relationships in order to establish the best opportunities for success?

PARTICIPANTS

Lee Hamilton (member of Congress, retired)
James A. Baker, III (Reagan)
Thomas McLarty (Clinton)
Donald Rumsfeld (Ford)
John Sununu (Bush)

KEYSTONE TASKS

MR. HAMILTON: The topic is starting the White House. What is the most important job of the chief of staff at the beginning of an administration?

MR. SUNUNU: Well, I think the most important job is to find out *what* the job is. The important thing to remember is that the role of a chief of staff is whatever the president wants that role to be. It is different in each administration. It may evolve during the administration, but until the chief of staff spends a little bit of time with the president to find out what the president wants, there's almost nothing you can do constructively to begin to fulfill the charge that you have from the person that you have to serve.

I think the second-most important thing to do is really to spend a little bit of time with others who have been in the job. I see people here who were kind enough to give me a lot of their time when I found out that I was going to have the responsibility of being chief of staff. It doesn't mean that you model the White House that the president has asked you to shape after any other administration, but there certainly are a great list of things you should do and especially things that you shouldn't do that come from the experience of people who have had that responsibility before.

MR. MCLARTY: I would agree with John's comments. Like him, I appreciate to this day the counsel and advice that I received from almost everyone in this room.

I think our challenge was to get a government in place after another party had held the White House for twelve years.[1] I think that's the beginning point of a new administration and a transition. I think, secondly, in our case it certainly was to bring immediate focus both publicly and internally to the economic plan and to get that plan developed consistent with presenting a budget, getting it passed and getting it communicated.

Also, in this painfully short period of transition one must make sure in the rush to get a government in place, and in our case to develop an economic plan and a budget, that there is a focus on national security issues and foreign policy even in the beginning of the inaugural activities and the transition.

Finally, in our case, I think it was also to integrate both the vice president [Al Gore] himself and the vice presidency into the administration. Of course, consistent with that is reaching out to members of Congress and members of the press.

MR. J. BAKER: I want to emphasize the fact that going to see the people who have been there before is extraordinarily valuable. I found that, frankly, to be a valuable experience before I took the job as secretary of state as well. One of the first things I did when I was asked to be chief of staff by President Reagan was to go sit down with Jack Watson and with Don Rumsfeld and with Dick Cheney and with one or two others. I got some very good ideas and some good signals as to where the landmines were. There are plenty of landmines in this job, probably more than almost any other job in Washington.

I also think it's important to make sure you understand what it is the president expects of you because there are any number of ways that the job can be structured. You can have a "spokes-of-the-wheel" arrangement where people can see the president and a number of people will have walk-in rights to the Oval Office or you can have a funnel where the chief of staff sits at the top. There are arguments with respect to all of these various ways to conduct the office.[2]

One of the most important things is to make sure you understand and have a clear understanding with the other people in the White House with respect to what everybody's roles are. That is particularly true, I think, with respect to the national security advisor. It is important that the administration functions as a unit. But you can't separate policy from politics in the White House and, therefore, it's important that the National Security Council work closely with the White House.[3]

And then transition is very, very important. We were very fortunate coming into the first Reagan term that Ed Meese, who had been President Reagan's chief of staff when he was governor of California, had spent a lot of time on transition planning.[4] We had a very smooth transition thanks to all the work that he did.

The last thing I would mention is to be sure that you have an effective first hundred-day plan. Every president gets a honeymoon. Sometimes it lasts a hundred days, sometimes it lasts less. Sometimes it lasts a little more. But, if you don't take advantage of that period, you are wasting some very valuable time.

MR. RUMSFELD: The most important responsibility of the chief of staff of the White House is to serve the president. The president's most important job, at the beginning of an administration, is bringing in the right people for the right jobs and giving them the right guidance and direction.

RECRUITING A STAFF

MR. HAMILTON: Let's consider the importance of getting the right people. I'd like you to comment a little bit on that, if you would. Is that among the most important tasks early on and to what extent does politics get into that? You have thousands of people that have worked for the president's election, many of them seeking a job, who want to get into the policy process. Talk a little bit about the intersection here of politics and getting the right people.

MR. SUNUNU: Let me make one point. A lot of what you end up finding out in reality is quite often counterintuitive. I don't think I've had any job in my life, and I haven't been able to hold them down too long so I've had a lot, that has more of that aspect to it, the counterintuitive nature. For example, Mack talked about the fact that they were an administration of a different party coming in. He suggested that that made it a little bit more difficult. Let me disagree with Mack on that.

I think it is much harder to have the administration of the same party make the transition because the expectations of everybody that is already in some position is that they will stay. That is a very difficult reality to deal with and to deal with it in a way that doesn't cost you all your political capital instantly is very, very hard. There is no question that in this job you better get used to spending political capital and you better make sure it is your own personal political capital that you're spending and not the president's political capital.

I often describe the role of the chief of staff with a very simple anecdote. If the secretary of state wants to have coffee with the president and the president doesn't want to have coffee the next day with the secretary of state and he doesn't mind the secretary of state knowing that he doesn't want him to have coffee, he tells him that he's not going to have coffee with him. But, if you get a call from the president saying "Will you tell the secretary of state I don't want to have coffee with him," it means tell him and don't let him know that I don't want to have coffee with him. That is the role of the chief of staff.

It is to say "No" in such a way that it is not the president saying "no" unless the president tells you that that's what he wants. It is being willing to take the grief and being artful enough to take the grief that's associated with it.

Going back to the beginning of the White House, also the same thing applies in terms of bringing good people in and replacing either people that thought they were going to stay, in the case of a like-party transition, or moving the pieces around in such a way that maximizes for the new president the talent that can be brought in to the White House without the accompanying ripples that are associated with bringing people in to slots and replacing other people.

MR. HAMILTON: Mack, what about this intersection of politics and people?

MR. MCLARTY: Well, I feel John's pain, but I still think after a vigorous campaign and expectations of those who had worked for a president and to have a Democratic president after twelve years, I think both of us had particular challenges in that regard.

I think we spent a lot of time focusing on the cabinet selection. And, Jim, I was fortunate to be part of that process on the selection even before I had fully accepted the position of chief of staff. So I felt a real sense of ownership and an ability to at least voice my views in that process, particularly on the economic team, which was critically important.

In terms of the White House staff, we did get to that late because of the lengthy cabinet process. I think that was a mistake. I think on the critical areas, however, in the White House, the National Economic Council was particularly critical to our administration and the security aspects, the national security team and even the domestic policy team, they were relatively in place. The economic team was not but I think we made some good choices there, both in the cabinet and in the White House. But I do think it was a misjudgment not to get an earlier start on the White House team.

MR. HAMILTON: Where do you look for people? The campaign? Washington? Where do you go?

MR. RUMSFELD: The search for good people is multifaceted. A number of fine people who are involved in the campaign offer their services. A great many other people write in, sending in their resumes. Many people recommend their friends and people they know. A great many people who come into the government know people that they have worked with previously. Capitol Hill is always a source of prospects. One of the best techniques is to ask three or four top experts in a given area and ask them for the best people they know of. When someone's name comes up several times, you may have a good prospect.

MR. J. BAKER: When you are replacing an administration of the other party, you look to the campaign more often than not to get the people that are going to come into the White House.

There is a body of career people in the White House. One of the best pieces of advice I got from Don Rumsfeld and Dick Cheney was to keep those people, don't think about moving them around, don't worry about their politics; they're basically apolitical; they know their jobs, keep them.

The main people that you bring on are the political appointees and most of those, in my experience, came out of the campaign. I think that's true with respect to the Reagan campaign in 1980 and the Bush campaign in 1988.

CRITICAL AUTHORITY

MR. HAMILTON: When you start, did you sit down with the president and have a clear understanding with the president of what your authority was going to be, what your responsibility was going to be? Did the president make that clear to you?

MR. RUMSFELD: Yes, indeed. It is important to have a clear understanding with the president as to your responsibilities. It is difficult early in an administration, particularly in the case of President Ford, who had not run for office or been elected.[5]

MR. J. BAKER: Well, I did in my case in 1980, because I was, after all, sort of an outsider coming into a group of Californians and I wanted to have a fairly clear understanding of what was expected of me and what was not expected of me and what my rights and obligations were. So, when President-Elect Reagan asked me to be his chief of staff, I sat down with Ed Meese who had been his chief of staff in California and whom we all knew was going to come into the White House in some major capacity. He and I worked out a division of responsibilities on a small piece of paper which I still have and took it in to the president, the president agreed to it and that was pretty much how we divided our respective responsibilities.

MR. SUNUNU: Of course you have that conversation. I didn't have the situation Jimmy did where Ed Meese and [Michael] Deaver and Jim had to make some delineation amongst themselves on the responsibilities. I had been governor of New Hampshire. It's certainly not the same role as president but, as governor, you know what you want your chief of staff to do and what you don't want them to do. So I came with that sense of the difference between the staff position of chief of staff and the responsibility of the chief executive. Certainly, that was part of the conversation that I had with the president.

Basically, this is the one area that you have to remember is both constant and evolves throughout your tenure. It's constant in the sense that the fundamental rule applies all the time and that is "No freelancing," that the chief of staff is there to do what the president wants. That may change and you have to change with it. You just have to get accustomed to the fact that, when in doubt, you go and ask. That was basically the formula President Bush worked with.

We had a morning meeting in which we talked about everything that we thought might come up during the day and I found out what he wanted or didn't want. We had a late afternoon meeting in which we reviewed the day and made sure what he wanted had gotten done. During the day, about two or three or four dozen times, I would walk down the hall on either the most significant matter or the most trivial matter to find out what he wanted done. You better pay attention to asking even on the trivial matters because those are probably the ones that end up costing you dearly because you made an assumption that really wasn't correct.

Yes, you have that meeting and, yes, you adjust it constantly as things evolve. When we got involved in the Gulf War, there was a slight deferral, if you will, of focus on some issues and yet you have to make sure that you bring those issues to the president periodically to get a fresh feeling and you don't let one crisis item tend to create in you a feeling that you already know what he wants and, therefore, you don't have to talk to him about it. You really have to refresh it constantly.

MR. MCLARTY: We had one initial conversation and two subsequent conversations and discussions during the transition where you do reach at least a framework of an agreement. Unlike perhaps like some have thought, I had never worked for Governor Clinton. I had never worked in his administration, despite a lifelong friendship, other than just as an outside kitchen cabinet type of advisor. I had also not been a formal part of the campaign. So I thought it was critical to get a very clear understanding to the extent and detail that you could. I agree with John. You set a framework and it evolves over time with the working relationship and the circumstances that you find yourself [in] and challenges and priorities.

But I found it relatively easy to reach agreement. We didn't really have any sharp points of disagreement or difference in point of view. I think access is critical and, frankly, just really the authority.

MR. HAMILTON: Mack, what do you mean by setting a framework?

MR. MCLARTY: Well, framework basically means what do you want, how do you want your chief of staff to function, because I think it very much reflects the personality and style of the president. Secondly, you have to have a clear understanding about access and that no major decision, hopefully no decision at all, will be made without at least your knowledge if not a strong ability to manage that process, access to the Oval Office, those types of things and, frankly, hiring and firing. We reached agreement on the hiring, that it would be a collaborative process, that I would have veto. And, on firing, in the end the president would respect my wishes on that.

MR. J. BAKER: Lee, let me just jump in there for one minute. I think

Mack has raised a point that's really important and that's to find a way to make sure that you can avoid the "Oh, by the way . . ." decisions. Everybody wants to get a decision from the president. I don't care how high ranking they are in the cabinet. They'll buttonhole the president after a cabinet meeting and say, "Mr. President, I'm going to do such and such." The president, of course, has a thousand things coming at him and he says, "Sure, fine." If you don't know about it, that's a recipe for trouble. So you really need to have an arrangement with the boss that no decisions are taken, nothing happens that you don't know about.

We had a system in the first Reagan term where any cabinet officer that wanted to see the president could see him on no less than twenty-four hours notice and usually a lot less than that. He had a P.O. Box where people could write him.[6] These things would go around the staff but he had agreement with us that anything that was brought up to him he would tell us about, he would debrief us on. He was very, very faithful to that agreement. So, we were able to avoid what could have been some problems in that first term. You have to be very careful about "Oh, by the way" decisions.

MR. SUNUNU: Not to overplay that remark, but that is really the issue that either creates or avoids more problems than anything else. President Bush was very, very good about making sure that he dealt with the communication back into the staff structure through the chief of staff. He had been around the White House enough as vice president to see the kind of difficulties that can create.

I would suspect that most of the major problems in any White House stem from a breakdown of that aspect of the relationship or the process that's in place.

MR. MCLARTY: I think Secretary Baker has comforted Leon [Panetta], Erskine [Bowles] and me. We thought it was only our president who said, "Oh, by the way, I agreed to this." I think there was one other point, at least in my case, and that is when you feel that you need to express a very strong point of disagreement with the president. How do you bring him either bad news or, more directly, how do you convey criticism to your president and your boss?

In my case, with a lifelong friendship and never having worked with or for him directly, I wanted to make sure we had a clear understanding of that. I didn't want to get, as Howard Baker told me, the worst job in Washington and lose a lifelong friend in the process. That did not seem like a win-win situation. So, I wanted to get a clear understanding on that. I did and I can truthfully say that part was a manageable part. The president was very good about that with me and I think with others in the White House.

MR. SUNUNU: Can I disagree with both Mack and Secretary Baker? I don't think it's the worst job in Washington. I have to tell you, I think it was a job that I had as much fun in and enjoyed as much as any job I've ever had in my life. I really mean that. I don't want to discourage future candidates for the job. It really is as satisfying and as gratifying a job as I can imagine having. I really think it's the second best job in Washington.

SETTING THE AGENDA

MR. HAMILTON: One of the responsibilities of the chief of staff is to make sure the president's agenda gets implemented. Who sets that agenda? The president, of course, sets it primarily, but what's your job?

MR. J. BAKER: Well, when you're an incoming administration, the agenda generally is set in the campaign, what are the president's primary policy goals as articulated in the campaign. In the case of the Reagan administration coming in during 1981 an agenda was contained in a hundred-day plan, which we spent some time crafting. It was focused on the economic aspects of President Reagan's campaign and policy agenda, reducing the top marginal tax rates from seventy down to something reasonable, deregulating the economy, getting the economy going again and so forth. We stuck to that pretty faithfully even to the point of having some tensions within the administration as to whether or not we were neglecting some national security issues that some thought we should have focused on.

MR. HAMILTON: Did you ever say to the president, "This ought to be on the agenda?" In other words, did you try to influence the president?

MR. J. BAKER: No. What we did say was, "This ought to be on the agenda" in terms of *who* should we see, who should we be *lobbying* on the Hill, what public liaison *activities* should we be doing, what should our communications plan be, that kind of thing. But the hundred-day plan was something that was developed during the transition. The president, himself, spent a lot of time on it, as a matter of fact. So, it was there in the plan. We had a road map and I think that is extraordinarily important.[7]

It's much more difficult to keep the president's policy agenda going after you've been there for a while, particularly when you have strong cabinet officials, all of whom want their share of presidential time and attention and resources and want to concentrate on what they think is the most important thing in terms of maintaining western civilization as we know it. And they all feel very strongly about it. You have to make sure working with the president that you keep the focus where it ought to be because there are only so many hours of the president's time.

MR. SUNUNU: And there are milestone situations. Certainly, the agenda is established, first of all, in the campaign. Whether you like it or not, you make campaign promises and that creates a framework for the agenda. Then the transition, in the transition you select from those commitments what you want to focus on in the first hundred days, the first congressional session, in fact, and that defines the agenda.

Then you have the milestones that are almost there on an annual basis, the State of the Union Address and the budget presentation, which allow you to update and recraft the presidential agenda. The president has certain strong ideas as to what he wants focused on in the State of the Union Address, in the presentation of the budget. You then go out and gather with whatever process you've established new, fresh ideas to add to that. So this is a process that is defined in the campaign, firmed up in the first hundred-day plan that you put together, and reestablished, redefined, and revitalized on an annual basis as you go through these cycles.

So there's lots of opportunity there for bringing items on to the agenda or taking items off if they have become stale.

MR. MCLARTY: Ours was straightforward. It did come off the campaign. It was "the economy, stupid," the phrase.[8] It was clearly an economic focus coming in. I think the other theme of the campaign was one of change. I think over 60 percent of the American people voted for change, but I felt, and I think the president agreed on most issues, they voted for thoughtful change, not radical or dramatic change. I think the other aspect coming in, ours was probably reflected in legislative initiatives in some measure, not only the economic plan but also an executive order with the Family Medical Leave Act, which I think sent the signal of balancing work and family, very much again connecting to the campaign, and then international economics with the passage of NAFTA [North American Free Trade Agreement] at the end of the year. Those were the first three major items on our agenda.

MR. J. BAKER: I think it's really important to keep focused on the fact that the chief of staff is a staff job. The people who wouldn't return your telephone calls *before* you became White House chief of staff are not going to return them *after* you end up your tenure. You tend to lose perspective when you're in there. It's very easy to do. You're somewhat isolated and you're extraordinarily powerful. You get fifty invitations a week to various things. Those invitations are not coming to you because you're who you are. They're coming to you because of your office. It's awfully easy to lose sight of that fact. I think that's an important element in doing the job right and something that we ought to make sure that the next occupant of the job understands.

MR. RUMSFELD: The president sets the agenda, using the staff and cabinet to assist him in fashioning priorities and specific substantive direction.

CONNECTING TO CONGRESS

MR. HAMILTON: You have a lot of people out there you have to deal with. You have the cabinet officials, you have interest groups, [and] you have the press. I'd like you to talk about each of those but let's start with the Congress. How do you relate to members of Congress?

MR. SUNUNU: Well, if I remember the numbers correctly, President Bush had a Congress in which 174 members of the House were Republicans and 45 members of the Senate. He had the smallest numbers of any president in the modern presidency and, therefore, the largest numbers of the opposite party. With all due respect to two people that have become very good friends of mine, Tom Foley and George Mitchell were extremely partisan as Speaker of the House and Majority Leader in the Senate. It was a very tough time. But the president really had an agenda on legislation, and that really is where this works the most, that was really broad and, in spite of perception, rather successful.

This is a president that took a stalemated Clean Air bill and got it passed. He had his own views on what he wanted in energy deregulation and got that passed. He had some ideas on agriculture reform that we implemented without hurting the family farmer. We got that passed. He had some ideas for restructuring the budget process. We got that passed. [He had] firm ideas on what the Americans with Disabilities Act ought to look like and we got that passed. The Civil Rights Bill, he got that passed. He has about ten major pieces of domestic legislation that he drove and got passed. Contrary to the perception, he probably has had more major successful domestic legislation gotten passed by Congress under the difficult circumstances that were there but the broadest domestic package of legislation of any president except Lyndon Johnson's Great Society packages. So, in spite of the perception that we were at loggerheads with Congress, we worked it very well. I hope it will be seen in the history of it, because this was a president that was willing to pick up the phone. So, you get the president to use all his resources. You certainly have a staff structure in there that works the Congress all the time. Then you try and coordinate. You can't be as successful as you'd like but you try and coordinate the interactions of the cabinet secretaries in dealing with Congress. You try and identify all the assets you have and all the relationships that you have and allocate responsibilities of working with Congress to different people because, frankly, the most important ingredient in dealing with Congress is probably identifying as many as possible personal relationships that you can call on at any given time.[9]

MR. HAMILTON: John, did you do a lot of calling to members of Congress as chief of staff?

MR. SUNUNU: Yes. I would say that a great portion of my responsibility was going up and dealing with Congress. We recognized because of the numbers that one of the things we had to establish was a capacity to have a credible veto. If George Bush did not have a credible veto, there is no way he could have influenced legislation.

While I was there, the president had no veto overridden. I think afterwards in the waning days of the administration, they had one veto overridden on a cable bill. But he has the best record of veto sustaining of any president and it's because we had a deliberate policy of establishing that beachhead in order to give credibility to the president saying "I will not accept legislation unless it has . . ." So, you have to do both, the stroking on the personal side but you do have to establish a mechanism for a credible line drawing that allows you to complement that.

MR. MCLARTY: In our case, of course, the president had run as a governor and not from the Congress itself. And, again, our focus was so much on the economic plan going in. We tried to establish early relationships with the leadership, with George Mitchell and with Tom Foley. We had thin majorities to say the least and the president had run as a "New Democrat," as a centrist, which was not fully reflective, I think, of many Democratic members of Congress and perhaps the majority in some ways. So, that was a balance that had to be achieved.

It was also critical, I think, to develop public support for what we were trying to pass where that resonated in individual districts and in individual states. And we were fortunate, particularly from the economic standpoint, to have Lloyd Bentsen as secretary of the treasury, Leon [Panetta] at OMB [Office of Management and Budget], people of standing that had worked in both the House and the Senate.[10]

MR. SUNUNU: Let me add one point. One of the most difficult things we had to do in dealing with Congress, and the president played the key role and defined how he wanted it done and who had to go out and do it, and Secretary Baker was up to his eyeballs in it, was getting the vote from Congress for the Gulf War.[11] You certainly remember how difficult—it wasn't so hard on the House side but certainly on the Senate side. The numbers I think we started with were about 35 or 37 votes that we could count on and eventually it moved up to 52. For each of the additional votes, we can have an anecdote about the personal relationship that generated it. I really do feel that working with Congress depends on identifying those personal relationships and, in the tough times, utilizing them.

MR. RUMSFELD: As a former member of Congress, it is of course much easier to relate to members. It is not an accident that Article I of the Constitution is the legislative branch. They have an important role to play and the executive branch needs to recognize that and stay in close touch with members.

MR. J. BAKER: There are a lot of egos up there on the Hill. The point that both of these guys made, I think, is absolutely valid. You need to spend a lot of time with Congress. You need to pony up to them and be nice to them. I never left the office at night that I did not at least return every congressional call I had. It was an easy way to get the call returned. You knew they'd gone home and you just left word that you were returning their call, but it pays off.

But, beyond that, the point that John made about an effective veto strategy is very valid. We were able to move things in the early days of the first Reagan term against a Democratically controlled House and Senate because we were able to roll them a couple of times. You have to be nice and you have to play to those egos but the most effective thing you can do is occasionally beat them on a vote. If you do that one or two times, they will pay attention. But you have to pick your shots pretty carefully because, if you try to do it and you lose, it's ten steps backwards.

MR. MCLARTY: Also, I think it depends on the legislation itself. In the economic plan, as diligently as we tried, we could not develop a bipartisan consensus. On NAFTA [North American Free Trade Act] we had a strong bipartisan effort. So I think it depends some on the legislative issue.

CONNECTING WITH THE PRESS

MR. HAMILTON: Let's talk about the press a little bit. What is the best way to deal with the press?

MR. SUNUNU: Well, I probably did the lousiest job of dealing with the press that any chief of staff has ever done and I acknowledge that. Partly it is because I tried very hard not to background the press and not to do things off the record with the press. I wanted really all of my discussions with the press to be on the record and, in retrospect, I probably shouldn't have done that. But I thought that I was doing that out of loyalty to a president that really loathed leaks and perceived that kind of briefing as being in that context. So, I acknowledge that that was probably something that I didn't appreciate until well out of the White House.

I will say that there is an art form to it and, to a great extent, a presidency gets defined by its handling of the press. I personally feel that part of the perception of George Bush as being a president that focused only on foreign policy in spite of all the tremendous success he had on domestic legislation is because the White House Press Office loved to brief on foreign policy but sent all domestic briefings over to the agencies. With all due respect, I think that had a very bad impact on the president. If I could go back and change any policy decision, I would implore the press office to change that policy decision and I'd go back and work the president harder to ask him to see that that was not in his best interest.

MR. MCLARTY: In my case, unlike Secretary Baker and Governor Sununu to some extent, I had to develop relations with the press. Unlike members of Congress, whom I had worked with for probably twenty years in the private sector, and members of the cabinet, many of whom I had known and so forth, other than the business press, I had not really established personal relationships with members of the Washington press corps. Of course, you, again, had Governor Clinton coming into Washington from a governorship, not from the Congress. So, that was a real challenge from our standpoint. I think the press does define in large measure what you're trying to do and I think, also, we were coming off the campaign where you had had coverage of the campaign and now you had coverage of the administration. That's quite a different perspective in many ways.

I think expectations have evolved a little bit so it's probably expected more now that the chief of staff is a little more out front in terms of the press than in prior years. Perhaps it's the news cycle and other things but I think that's expected now. I would argue more toward interface with the press and even on background and certainly in terms of public appearance. Not getting out too far, I'm not suggesting that, but probably more proactive than in past years.

MR. RUMSFELD: Generally, the cabinet and press secretary are the people that deal with the press. Needless to say, there are many times when the chief of staff must deal with the press. Generally, that is on background but there are occasions when it is important for the chief of staff to be more visible, but those occasions should be rare.[12]

MR. J. BAKER: You're well aware of the old saying: "The higher the monkey climbs, the more you see of his behind." The White House chief of staff's job is a big target to begin with. If you get too visible in that role, you're going to have trouble.

I really want to make the distinction here in case it's lost on anybody between "backgrounding" and "leaking." Leaking is talking to the press in an effort to drive a personal agenda or revealing information to the press that you have no right to reveal about the administration or the president or some of your opponents in the administration. Backgrounding is talking to the press in order to spin the administration's line and drive the administration's policy. I think it's a very critical element of the chief of staff's job.

REACHING INTEREST GROUPS

MR. HAMILTON: Okay. One other group, special interest groups, lobbying groups. How did the chief of staff relate to these groups?

MR. RUMSFELD: Interest groups are part of one's constituency. It is important to have relationships with key interest groups across the spectrum.

MR. SUNUNU: You know one of the roles of the chief of staff is to not only be willing to catch the spears that come close to the president but, frankly, I think you wake up every morning and try and decide where you're going to stand in order to catch [them]. You have to anticipate it. The greatest attacks I think that a president takes are not from partisan criticism that might come from members of the Congress or whatever it is but these constituency groups who rally rumblings to either pass or influence policy one way or the other. They really do have a surprisingly effective reach back into the hinterland and they do start spinning things in a way that creates a difficulty for the president and the White House. I really do think that one of the important roles of the chief of staff is to make sure that if there is any anger toward the White House that it's focused toward the chief of staff and not the president.

We had a very difficult time with the savings and loans. Everybody involved in real estate and the banking business was sure that all the president had to do was write one magic executive order and turn the real estate and savings and loan situation around. In spite of the fact that we would bring in—I'm using this as an example—folks involved in that by a dozen or so to talk at the White House and in spite of the fact that we would always ask the question "And what do you want the president to do?" and in spite of the fact that you never got a single recommendation of anything that could be done, they would all go back and say that the White House is just not doing what it should do. One of the things you have to do is you try and get the communication going but in those cases where it is impossible to resolve, where you cannot get Treasury, for example in this case, to placate in terms of policies that they see are moving in the right direction or get the process moving or whether the time constant for change is so long, one of the things you better do as chief of staff is make sure that the president is protected somehow. Quite often it really does mean that you have to stand there and point to the target on your chest and say "throw it here."

The other thing you have to do is give equal access and create a balanced perception and let people on both sides of an issue feel that they are having access. One of the things that was publicized when I came in as an Arab American chief of staff was that the Jewish American community was a little concerned that an Arab American was going to be chief of staff. After I had been out of there for about three months, one of the nice things is that four or five members of the Jewish American liaison group called me up and said, "Holy smokes, we've lost our access. Come back."

MR. J. BAKER: It's another important element of the chief of staff's job. You have a whole component of the staff structure within the White House that deals with public liaison and you use or try to use those groups to advance the president's agenda, and you certainly try and stay on good terms with them.

ADVISING THE PRESIDENT

MR. HAMILTON: We're going to go to the audience here for questions in just a minute, but let me just ask one question that I hope is not out of bounds. If you sensed that the president was wrong on an issue, how did you deal with it? Or did that ever occur?

MR. MCLARTY: In my case, if you felt the president was either wrong or was moving in a direction that was going to create a problem or a mistake, I generally dealt with it one on one. I would seek, depending on the subject matter, advice and counsel from people I really trusted, generally within the White House, to be sure I was viewing the situation right before I would raise an issue with the president in such a direct manner. But I did it on several occasions, always one on one in the Oval Office, always with respect. It worked well. The president took criticism well or took a different point of view.

MR. HAMILTON: Were you successful?

MR. MCLARTY: Sometimes I was and sometimes I was not. It doesn't mean I was always right either.

MR. SUNUNU: Again, it depends on the president's style. I worked for a president where there were lots of one-on-one opportunities and you don't let something get to a point where it is so egregious you just have to say it's wrong. You are exchanging ideas on issues that are critical to the president and you are voicing your opinion throughout the process so you never get to the point, at least I never had to get to the point, where it was an abrupt "in my best opinion, sir, you are wrong." It is always giving feedback back and forth.

As Secretary Baker knows, through all the process where things were important with George [H. W.] Bush, he sat three, four, five, six of us down and he expected us to take both sides of an issue and tell him what was good about something and what was bad about something. He was a great absorber of both sides of an issue and then when he came to a decision you had the confidence that he had heard both sides and you almost never got to that situation where there was an abrupt discussion that had to take place.

MR. J. BAKER: I think one of the most important functions you can perform for your president is to be willing to give it to him with the bark off. You have to be willing to go in there and say, "I really disagree with that, sir," or "I don't think that's the way we ought to go." You'll win some of those and you'll lose some of them but that is one of the most important things that you have to do for your president. The worst chief of staff I think would be a "yes man" who was never willing to tell the president what his views were or what he thought. I found it to be the case that, if you felt strongly enough about it, you would go enlist other allies and try and get the president to come around, not least of which would be the first lady in both the administrations that I worked in, one as chief of staff and one as secretary of state, or other people. I think it's really important to do that.

I'm going to tell a story about Dick Cheney, which I hope he won't mind. I remember an instance in the Ford administration when Dick was chief of staff and I was chairman of the President Ford Committee. Actually at that time I was the delegate hunter for President Ford. We were engaged in a really tough fight with Governor Reagan for the nomination. An incumbent president was about to be knocked off by the governor of California.

Secretary [of state Henry] Kissinger had been on a very successful mission to some country in either Africa or South America. I can't remember which. But Henry at that time was not particularly popular with the

Republican right. President Ford thought that Henry had done a great job on this mission so he said, "We're going to have him brief the White House press in the press room." I called Dick from the campaign and said, "Dick, you can't let this happen one week in advance of the Texas primary where we're having such trouble. You simply can't let that happen."

And Cheney tells me, he says, "Look, I've already broken my pick. If you feel so strongly about it, you go in there."

So, I went in there and told President Ford I thought this was a terrible mistake and President Ford said, "Jim, Henry's done a wonderful job. Anyway, the thinking Republican voters of Texas will understand this."

I said, "Mr. President, I hate to tell you this but, on this issue, there are no thinking Republican voters in Texas." But he didn't change his mind . . .

MR. RUMSFELD: With a president like President Ford, the answer to the question as to how to deal with the president when you believe he is wrong on an issue: you simply tell him. And tell him why. He was a well-centered person as president and a pleasure to work with.

AUDIENCE QUESTIONS

MR. LAZARUS: Richard Lazarus. I'm here at the Wilson Center and on the faculty at Georgetown University.

Secretary Baker, you mentioned when you took the White House chief of staff job you talked to some former White House chiefs of staff, I think Jack Watson and Don Rumsfeld and maybe also Mr. Cheney. They talked to you about the landmines that were there. If you were advising the next administration coming in and let's say, to make it easier, George W. Bush wins, and the new chief of staff calls you up, what would be the landmines that you would tell them or, should I say, who would be the landmines?

MR. J. BAKER: Well, some of the ones that I've already mentioned, Richard. The "Oh, by the way" decisions; the idea that you should be not overly seen or heard in that job; that you should pick the right people; that you should understand that your responsibility is to help formulate but particularly implement the president's policy agenda administration-wide. These are the things that I would refer to as landmines. Be sure that you, for instance, cultivate the press properly, that you cultivate the Congress properly, that you cultivate the public liaison groups properly, those kinds of things.

MR. LAZARUS: What about the first lady?

MR. J. BAKER: Well, the first lady, you want to make sure that you don't hang up on her when she telephones you, you bet your life. That is a fundamental mistake. You don't want to do that. Fortunately, none of us here did that, did we?[13]

[laughter]

MR. SUNUNU: There are some other things that don't sound significant that you learn. One of the things that I think is important that I would convey to the next generation would be that you have to recognize that there is a tendency in the White House for people to think that they have to work twenty-four hours a day, seven days a week only to show how important they are. Whether they acknowledge that or not, there's that psychological instinct.

One of the things that I did after having talked to the president was really discourage people from coming in and working on Sunday. Frankly, you try to keep them out of there Saturday afternoon too. The reason is there's no question you're going to get 15, 20 percent more efficiency the other six days a week if they've got a chance to go and take care of their personal needs and their family needs. But there's a second more important reason for that and that is, when a real crisis comes along, if you have not established that kind of a working structure, you have no slack in the system to deal with a crisis.

It's one of the things that we implemented; it's the small item that I think made a big difference. It created a better working environment. It created a better tone, a better set of relationships. Certainly we had a president that wanted a White House to feel good about working there and didn't want to create family impacts. George Bush was probably the easiest president to work for that I can imagine in terms of understanding the personal needs of the staff that were there, and it made a big difference.

MR. RUMSFELD: The chief of staff has been not inaccurately characterized here as a "javelin catcher." There really are no landmines, however. Most of the mistakes that human beings can make have been made, and if one takes a look at history, they will see a lot of potholes in the road up ahead that they could, with a little thought, avoid. It is not easy, but it can be done.

MR. KONDRACKE: Morton Kondracke. Two things. First, my impression is that when the Clinton administration came in they found no records, no hard drives on computers. Nothing seemed to work. There was no historical memory. I just wonder whether—Jay Leno called it Chinese carryout. But seriously, is that going to happen when the next administration comes in, that there is no data there?

Secondly, the question of appointments. I know one current cabinet officer who had a fairly simple financial background, had to spend $20,000 on accountants to put her records in shape in order to present to do the financial filings. Now, has that been corrected?

MR. SUNUNU: No.

MR. MCLARTY: The answer to the last question, to my knowledge it has not been corrected. I think there has been a lot of discussion. I think, Howard, you've been approached and a number of others have about some type of commission to look at financial records and the vetting process. To my knowledge it has not been simplified. I believe in the near term it probably will not be although I think it should be.

On the transition itself, I certainly shouldn't speak and won't speak for the current administration but I would hope that they would make a serious effort to have a good transition, a helpful transition with whichever candidate is elected.

Certainly, I think, Jim, you and your staff with Andy Card and Bob Zelleck and others were enormously helpful to us in the transition. There may have been some administrative and technical things such as the hard drives that were problematic, but certainly, from my standpoint and my immediate staff's standpoints, the transition was a good one.

MR. J. BAKER: Well, we had a good transition too thanks to help from Hamilton Jordan and Jack Watson when we came in, in 1981.[14] We had a good transition primarily, and I think I mentioned this a little bit earlier, because Ed Meese and others had the foresight to really get a process going on the transition even during the campaign.

Now, that's very dangerous because it tends to have people say you're assuming you're going to win; it's arrogance and it has a negative political connotation. But there is some legislation I note that's being proposed now that suggests or that recommends that both campaigns openly engage in transition planning during the election. And that would be really helpful, Mort, to getting off to a good start, particularly when you're changing from one party to another.

MR. SUNUNU: There's been an evolution in this city in which I really do think people are beginning to understand that you don't get in trouble for doing something wrong. You get in trouble for doing something right in a way that somebody makes look as if you did something wrong. I think you're going to find a trend toward—and I'm talking about this now as a problem for historians. You're going to find a trend in which the written record, the magnetic record, disappears. Not that anyone has done anything that they are ashamed of or is improper or not correct but they just don't want to create an opportunity for mischief for whatever reason might be there. I am worried that the historical record is being impacted that way. That's why I think this is a very important forum.

That's why I think and I would urge those who understand the art of oral histories to recognize there are probably a cycle of oral histories you should plan for. One set of oral histories taken immediately after an administration leaves so that people will tell you in a fresh way everything they're willing to tell you at that time and then I'd schedule something maybe a half a dozen or a dozen years later and let them tell you all the rest. It may not be so fresh but it will fill in the blanks.

I am very concerned that the climate of what we have created in this city is such that the historical record is being impacted and that more than anything else is the concern that I would have of the kind of situation that might have been raised.

MR. J. BAKER: Let me second what John has said. You saw that climate being created back beginning, I suppose, in the late seventies but it really, really was exacerbated during the eighties and nineties. We didn't keep any written notes. By the time we got to the Bush administration, I stopped writing anything down. Why? Because everything was subject to subpoena, everything. And that is going to impact the historical record. Even though we've gotten rid of the independent counsel law, which was a very wise thing to do, it's still "gotcha" politics in this city. Politics is extraordinarily ugly today. It's almost remarkable that people will continue to offer themselves for public service either electorally or from an appointive standpoint because you subject yourself to the possibility of really unjust allegations and accusations. Until we get away from the idea that the best way to win is to get your opponent indicted, we're going to have this problem with maintaining a historical record of governance.

MR. MAIER: Peter Maier with CBS News. I'm wondering if you could elaborate on the pros and cons on having a chief of staff who is a best buddy who goes back many years, as Mr. Mclarty did, or someone who did come in as an outsider, by and large, as Governor Sununu and Secretary Baker did in some cases?

MR. SUNUNU: I think you need both. I think that in spite of Secretary Baker being perceived as being an outsider at the time, he had been in the city a while and people who knew the president well knew Jim Baker well. So, if it wasn't a one-on-one personal friend relationship, it was a relationship where he could be identified as being a friend, and that is important.

I came as a governor from outside the city but, over the six years of being a governor, I had developed a very good personal relationship with the president. In my opinion, there is no way a president should select a chief of staff that he is not comfortable or she is not comfortable enough with to have that chief of staff go in and do what Jim Baker said was one of the most important things and that was say, "Mr. President, you are wrong." You need a relationship in which that can be done by the chief of staff. If there is a litmus test in the mind of a president, it is you must select somebody from whom you are willing to take that kind of a comment, all other things being appropriate in terms of experience, political sense, and understanding.

MR. RUMSFELD: It doesn't matter if the individual is an old friend or not. What's important is that the president has confidence in the individual, the individual is capable of doing the job, and the individual has interest in seeing that the president is a success.

MR. MCLARTY: I think the personal relationship is very important and I think, particularly at the beginning of an administration, it is probably a different kind of relationship than as the administration evolves. In my case, as I noted before, while having a lifelong friendship, I had never served with Governor Clinton. I think the basis for that was someone not unlike what John just said. It's someone where there was a level of trust and respect, particularly in the early going, that could have a sense of are you seeing this correctly or not and had the ability to say, "I disagree with you," or "You need to think about it this way or that way."

I think also it depends on the period of the emphasis you're going to have. In our case, it was the economic plan going in. Of course, I was from the business community.

MR. J. BAKER: I think John Sununu has it exactly right on that. It needs to be someone who will say, "You're wrong, Mr. President. I really don't think this is the right thing to do." You do need that whether it's a lifelong friend or whether it's someone else. It's also helpful to have someone who knows how this city operates. Beyond that, you want to pick somebody who has the other talents that go with the job. But I don't think it's an either/or situation.

MR. WEBSTER: Scott Webster, Harvard University. What authority or power or responsibility did you have that you most wish you didn't have or that perhaps you even resented or wish wasn't part of your bailiwick as chief of staff?

MR. RUMSFELD: I can think of no responsibility I had that I wished I didn't have. The chief of staff has so many things to do that it is pretty easy to delegate anything that is not appropriate for the chief of staff to be doing.

MR. SUNUNU: I wouldn't wish not to have it but the most unpleasant part of the job was having to tell somebody they were fired. I had a very difficult one. I had a very close friend from Tufts University who was secretary of education, Secretary [Lauro] Cavazos, whom I had known for years, had been secretary of education in the Reagan administration and whose focus had been as dean of the dental school at Tufts. His focus was really higher education and the president wanted to focus on K–12. It really was probably the toughest single thing I had to do as chief of staff. If you ask me to list things I wish I didn't have to do, that's the one that I would put up there. I probably don't have a second. That's the only one thing. And it was hard.

MR. MCLARTY: It's difficult in the private sector and it's equally difficult in the public sector. Very few of us like to terminate anyone particularly when they've given a serious good faith effort. I think the other authority and responsibility, and you know it's yours, is to make the decision knowing that you're going to step in front of the javelin, and that's your responsibility and you have the authority to do that. You have to make that decision and you know you did it, but you know that going in.

Notes

1. Mr. McLarty refers to the period 1981 through 1992, the presidencies of Ronald W. Reagan and George H. W. Bush.

2. For an assessment of these different models of White House organization, see Alexander L. George, *Presidential Decisionmaking in Foreign Policy: The Effective Use of Information and Advice* (Boulder, Colo.: Westview Press, 1980).

3. A product of the 1947 statute on national security apparatus, the National Security Council includes major representatives of the security and diplomatic agencies of the executive branch, such as State and Defense. The president chairs the National Security Council. The NSC maintains a staff of around 200 headed by the president's special assistant for national security affairs or "national security advisor" (NSA). Often, White House staffs consider the NSA as the "chief of staff" for international affairs, creating a tension between the NSA and the White House chief of staff.

4. Edmund Meese III served as counselor to President Ronald Reagan and director of policy development in the initial stages of the Reagan administration. Mr. Meese had served as governor of California Ronald Reagan's chief of staff and then his presidential campaign manager. As campaign manager, Meese directed the Reagan presidential transition planning effort. With James A. Baker, III, chief of staff, and Michael Deaver, deputy chief of staff, Mr. Meese made up the third leg of the Reagan White House "troika." In the second Reagan administration (1985–88), Mr. Meese served as attorney general.

5. Under the twenty-fifth amendment to the U.S. Constitution, President Richard Nixon nominated (and the Congress confirmed) Gerald R. Ford, then a member of Congress from Michigan and House Minority Leader, to replace former Vice President Spiro Agnew who resigned as part of a federal plea bargain. Later, when President Nixon resigned the presidency in August of 1974, Vice President Ford became the nation's only unelected president.

6. *Time Magazine*, Sept. 30, 1991, p. 19 reported the use of a similar mailbox in Maine for President George H. W. Bush to maintain contact with his cabinet without going through the chief of staff.

7. Richard Wirthlin, with the assistance of David Gergen, directed the development

of a detailed hundred-day plan for the Reagan administration. See the discussion of transition planning in "Assessing Transition 2001."

8. Mr. McLarty refers to a key slogan of the Clinton campaign in 1988, running against sitting president George H. W. Bush. During the last two years of the Bush presidency, the American economy suffered through a period of slow economic activity without much apparent action by the Bush administration. In a three-way race the two challengers, Democrat William Clinton and independent candidate H. Ross Perot, drew nearly 60 percent of the vote.

9. The Clear Air Act Amendments renewed and modified the nation's organic legislation authorizing federal government involvement in setting and regulating standards of air quality and air pollution. Americans for Disabilities Act (ADA) set as government policy fighting discrimination against disabled citizens. The most obvious elements of the act removed architectural barriers to the handicapped and outlawed employment practices that discriminated against the handicapped. The Civil Rights Act of 1964, the basic organic legislation regulating discrimination in commerce and public accommodations, was renewed during the Bush administration. The "Great Society" program of President Lyndon Johnson represents the high point of post–World War II presidential policy making.

10. Then–senior senator from Texas, Senator Bentsen had run as the Democratic nominee for vice president in 1988. Then–vice president George H. W. Bush was elected in 1988. Leon Panetta had served as a member of the U.S. House of Representatives from California. See also his biography in "Members of the Forum."

11. The Persian Gulf War resulted when forces from Iraq invaded and occupied the Kingdom of Kuwait in August of 1991. In a famous statement on the White House lawn, then-president George H. W. Bush promised "this aggression will not stand." By January of 1992, President Bush had amassed a significant coalition of nation-states determined to expel Iraq from Kuwait, which they did in a war that lasted only a couple of weeks. Congressional opponents to the military buildup necessary to expel Iraq argued in favor of extending and applying a series of worldwide economic sanctions designed to force Iraq out of Kuwait. Eventually, Congress passed a resolution of support for the president's actions and any military actions against Iraq.

12. In jargon about press relations, being "on background" means the press cannot attribute statements to you or give any information about your identity when quoting you. Background statements are juxtaposed with "on the record" statements and "off the record." As indicated by the participants, background statements usually help reporters gain insight into issues and events without revealing their sources of information. Background statements also allow for "spinning" stories, presenting what some would consider a controversial interpretation of events or developments.

13. Many believe that Reagan chief of staff Donald Regan developed major difficulties in his job by hanging up on First Lady Nancy Reagan, thereby angering her and poisoning his relationship with President Reagan.

14. Hamilton Jordan was campaign director and counselor to then-president Jimmy Carter. Jack Watson was President Carter's final chief of staff. See his biography in "Members of the Forum."

CHAPTER 3

Refocusing the White House

The demands placed on the president's staff, the character of the nerve center itself, make staff turnover inevitable. Often that change begins with the chief of staff. When a chief of staff leaves, the president finds someone new to take on the core functions of the White House, its organizational routines, its divided and probably sputtering operation, a likely crisis, and its inevitable tensions. The discussion in this section covers all of those issues. It includes the cast of former chiefs of staff who have taken on such a call to duty, when things have not gone well and the president needs help.

While this section covers many of the same issues as the discussion on transitions, such as recruitment and access, the focus here is on those issues in a new context: when authority and responsibility have no clear focus.

Appropriately enough, then, these discussions begin with the president's commitment on basic authority for a new chief of staff. Often that new authority lays the foundation for a reorientation of White House operations, to a new discipline and a new focus. These chiefs of staff discuss the sensitivity of change and how to properly make this difficult transition from old routines to new ones—a transition often as delicate as that first one, from old to new administration.

White House discipline, of course, begins with the White House staff. Some expect that a new chief facing tough times would best serve the president by "cleaning house," moving out experienced staff who have developed bad habits and replacing them with a White House staff attuned to the new circumstances and the new chief of staff. Others make clear that a new chief, especially one facing an imminent crisis, cannot afford to lose all of the expertise accumulated in experienced staff. These two sides of the problem present a variation on the dilemma of discipline: how can a new chief proceed to restore the president's fortunes and reorient the White House when so many have adapted to the chaos?

The executive branch provides another variation on the dilemma of discipline. The cabinet agencies, of course, perform policy functions parallel to the White House staff. Staff in the cabinet agencies and those in the National Security Council take up the slack when the central White House staff falters, partly to protect their own policy ambitions, entwined with the president's, and partly to exert their own initiative, where they have differed from the White House. The new chief of staff must reassert the role of the central White House staff and orchestration. How can these new chiefs recover their central position in the president's team? Many observers think that a chief's control and, hence, White House discipline, begins with the president's schedule. Where presidents face enormous temptations to rely on other executive branch actors, and where opportunities for "oh, by the way" decisions have multiplied in the vacuum, a new chief must gain control of the president's time and initiative. How can they do that?

Because of their experiences, the former chiefs of staff in this discussion have a range of insights into the nature of partisan crisis, the dilemma of effectiveness. Since each has come into office in the midst of some challenging situation, each has recommendations for how to wall off a crisis, gain control of its momentum, and restore White House routines. Since much of that focus begins with the president's own activities, scheduling again becomes the narrows a new chief must guard.

PARTICIPANTS

Bill Plante (CBS News)
Howard Baker, Jr. (Reagan)
Erskine Bowles (Clinton)
Leon Panetta (Clinton)
Samuel Skinner (Bush)

CRITICAL AUTHORITY

MR. PLANTE: The special context for this second session is coming in and taking over, most of the time after a perceived problem or difficulty. Most of the members of this panel were in the position of having to change things about the way the staff was working. So we will ask them to reflect on their experiences, the lessons they learned. We'll ask them how they functioned as they took over in midcourse.

You came to your jobs because there was a perceived need for change, whether there had been a slight bump in the road or perhaps a train wreck. Did the fact that there was this perceived need for change, that there were problems, give you any particular leverage with your president? Senator, let me ask you to begin.

MR. H. BAKER: Well, first of all, I'd like to suggest a division of the question. You came in and took over. Well, I certainly came in at I guess a crucial point in the Reagan administration but taking over was a much slower process, if indeed we ever did. I came in following Don Regan. He left abruptly. When I got there, there was literally nothing going on. I went to the White House and visited with President Reagan. We had a nice chat. I'll talk more about that perhaps. I told him what I planned to do then was to get my personal affairs in order and to be on duty on Monday—this was on Friday—and I went home.

About two hours later, I got a call from Dennis Thomas who was deputy to Don Regan. He said, "You can't wait until Monday." I said, "Why not?" He said, "Nobody's in charge and nobody is doing anything. Nobody knows what to do. And you can't wait until Monday. You have to come down now." So, I think I found Jim Cannon who was at the White House for a while and previously had been in the Ford administration, Tommy Griscom, who was my press secretary, and A. B. Culvahouse, who was to become White House counsel. I hadn't found Kenny [Duberstein] yet, but he paid for that as time went by. We went down to the White House and set in motion a temporary organization. It was both a daunting experience and a frightening experience in a way to come into the White House cold and have virtually no staff but, more important, not even to have an organizational chart, not to have an agenda, not to have a schedule for the president for the next week.

So, when we got there our first job was to figure out what happens next. I've gone on too long now but that was a very tough time and I must say President Reagan was absolutely superb. He understood the gravity of the situation and he offered me the latitude and flexibility that I might need to staff and to get things started at the White House, and we did that.

So my real experience as chief of staff did not begin for a few days after that when we finally figured out what goes on at the White House, who does what, who was going to stay, who was going to be replaced, the allocation of responsibilities and duties but, most of all, the president's schedule. The president cannot sit there and not have a schedule. So my first instruction to this small group that I had was build me a schedule for the next week for the president. They did that. It was a pretty arbitrary thing. Some of the stuff, looking back on it, was sort of nonsensical. But there were public events and we kept the president occupied in this schedule.

I took it in to him and I said, "Mr. President, I can't find your schedule for next week but I have a suggestion here." He looked at it and he looked up at me and said, "Okay." And that was his schedule. He became fully engaged then and he carried it out with the gravity of the negotiation of the end of World War II. It was a reassuring experience.

MR. PLANTE: Not to belabor the point, but did you feel the need—and I'd like all the panelists to address this—coming in under those kinds of circumstances to get any particular assurances from the president about what you'd be able to do?

MR. H. BAKER: Well, I probably shouldn't tell you, but when I first met the president, I never thought about being anybody's chief of staff. I really am a congressional type.[1] I served for a long time in the Senate and, let me say parenthetically, chief of staff is an exalted position but the best job in this town other than president of the United States is Majority Leader of the Senate. And that was sort of my mindset. He asked me if I had any immediate requirements to take over this job and I said, "Mr. President, just two things. One, give me a little time to find out what's going on." This was against the background and backdrop of Iran-Contra.[2] I said, "The other is I want to bring my own lawyer." And I did. I brought A. B. Culvahouse who was one of my law partners. He came to the White House and literally that was the only requirement I tried to place on the president and he was in total agreement.

MR. SKINNER: I had the unique situation in that we were in an election year. We announced our campaign organization and our government organization at the same time. We called everyone in and said, "You're going to do this. You're going to do that," and it was a structure that I don't think in a reelection effort has ever been set up since. I don't recommend it but with President Bush feeling that the campaign organization ought to be run outside the White House and the operations of government ought to be run inside and we ought to have two concurrent efforts going on, it was a unique situation.

As to the staffing issue, the president felt very strongly—and John had recruited a good, loyal staff of people, and the president felt very loyal to them. I must tell you that the night I met with the president in the East Wing, I did not feel that I was in a position to tell him my demands as to what I should give the president of the United States. I'm used to asking and negotiating but not with the president of the United States. I found it, frankly, a little intimidating. He needed to make a change. He wanted to make it quickly. We were at 40 percent in the polls and we were ten months away from an election. So I basically took the deck of cards and the hand that was dealt to me and worked with it.

Having said that, I think in the ideal situation you would want to make an arrangement with the president on staffing so that the two of you would have an understanding as to how the staffing would proceed and how the selection would proceed and that you would have people that were working for him and you that knew that they were there because you and the president had selected them. That would give them the kind of responsibility and loyalty. I made some changes that I probably shouldn't have made and I did not make some that I probably should have. I think that was a situation but I think it's unseemly to demand. You can have an understanding but it's not a demand. It's really a negotiation where the principal has the upper hand in the negotiation.

Also, I think the structure is very important. You certainly should have input into the structure because how you're going to operate within the White House is clearly something that you have to negotiate with the president so he's comfortable with it and you're comfortable with it. We were able to do that. There were a few things that were residual from previous administrations and, because President Bush had so many long-standing relationships with people, the issue of access and control of the schedule, there were a few exceptions to the rule but the chief of staff controlled the schedule and made sure that the right people got to him at the right time.

Going to Jim Baker's point, I also wanted to encourage people whom he had confidence in having access to him so that, number one, if they agreed with me, they would tell the president what I thought and what they thought and, number two, he wasn't so insulated or isolated in the White House that he wasn't really getting input from what was going on. But I think it's important that you negotiate the process as well as the people.

MR. PANETTA: I was very happy as the director of the Office of Management and Budget and I told the president that, as a matter of fact. I didn't have any sense that anything was really churning until actually Mack McLarty called me in and began to ask, "What would you do if you were chief of staff in terms of trying to develop a better organization within a White House?" I gave him my thoughts and I didn't think that much of it. Then on a trip to Europe for the Normandy celebration the president called me over and asked me if I had any thoughts about how to better reorganize the White House.[3]

I said, "I can give you some thoughts, but I think you're doing fine. I think Mack's doing fine. It's just a question of trying to tighten up on some of the operations."

Then I went back to being director of the Office of Management and Budget and I enjoyed the fact that there is a street that separates the Old Executive Office Building from the White House because you basically have your own operation there. I was walking across the street there to the White House and the vice president [Albert Gore] pulled me over and he said, "The president is seriously thinking of appointing you as chief of staff."

I said, "Well, I don't want it. I'm director of OMB. I'm enjoying the job. I think the president needs me in this position." We had just passed the economic plan. I was working all of the appropriations bills. I knew the budget.

And he said, "Yes, but the president really needs you."

The next thing I knew I was being called up to Camp David, to be present at Camp David with the president, the first lady, the vice president, and Tipper [Gore] all in one room. They said, "We need you to be chief of staff."

I said, "I'm very good at being director of OMB. You really need my experience. I've worked the budget. We've worked the economic plan. We've put it together. We've gotten it passed. That's our strength. You need to have me doing that."

And the president said, "Look, Leon, you can be the greatest director of OMB in the history of this country but, if the White House isn't working, nobody's going to remember you."

And I said, "All right. I'll do this."

But I also knew at the time that it was important to have several things in place and I asked this at the time. I said, "Number one, I need to have your trust." In the prior discussion, all of these elements that Jim Baker and others talked about are very important but fundamental to the relationship between a chief of staff and the president is trust. If you don't have trust, you can be the greatest chief of staff in the world and you're not going to get anything done because the president and you will not have the kind of relationship you need in order to fulfill that job. In my case, I didn't have a long-standing experience with the president that went back to Arkansas, but he respected my experience and he respected my views, certainly in terms of the budget, and building on that was extremely important. Since he respected my views, it didn't take us very long to develop that trust.

Secondly, I said, "You need to establish control." If you're going in for the first time, you have to establish control. The only way you can establish control is if the president is willing to give you the authority you need to bring on the staff, to move the staff, to hire and fire. So, I asked him, "I need to have that complete authority. I also need to have the support of you, Mr. President, the first lady and the vice president of the United States. I've got to have your total support in what takes place."

And lastly, of course, access. You have to make sure that you have full access so that when you are dealing with either policy issues or personnel issues, there's no question that you're going to have that kind of access. Those were the important things and I did lay these out at the time before I took it. The president, of course, obviously was very supportive as was the first lady and the vice president. Building on that relationship, you could then begin to do some of the work that had to be done to try to get the White House reorganized.

MR. PLANTE: You say you did lay those out in advance?

MR. PANETTA: Yes, I did.

MR. PLANTE: Erskine?

MR. BOWLES: I often felt that the change from the private sector to the public sector is very broad. I felt that going from the private sector to the SBA [Small Business Administration] for me was a change as stark as going from day to night. If I thought *that* was a change, going from the SBA to the White House was a sea change. I have often felt that I was lucky to begin my public sector career at the SBA, which is kind of like being way off Broadway where every little mistake you make doesn't end up on the front page of the *Wall Street Journal* or the *New York Times*. I found out pretty quickly when I got to the White House with Leon [Panetta] that every little mistake you make at the White House—even better, no sin or deed—goes unpunished or unpublished.[4] It's a unique environment to operate in.

I think I was lucky when I came back to the White House because I had had the experience of working for Leon for two years. So I knew the rhythm of a White House and I knew how it operated. I had also had the experience of operating another federal agency outside of the White House so I had that perspective I think, which helps you a great deal in knowing how to manage within this environment.

Thirdly, I'd had about six to nine months away from Washington to give me a perspective of how people viewed the administration. Lastly, I had had the chance during my work with Leon to see how a disruptive influence like a Dick Morris could come in to the White House and know that was something that I was not going to be able to tolerate if I was going to come back and be the chief of staff.[5]

So I felt my experience working for Leon, working in the administration gave me a chance to succeed that I couldn't have had if I had come straight out of the private sector. Secondly, I did sit down with the president and I did get absolute assurances that I could have the controls I think that every chief of staff needs to have a chance to succeed.

ADVISING THE PRESIDENT

MR. PLANTE: Coming in at the middle, did you find that you were in the position of having to renegotiate things, walk things back, cover for the president? For example, when the president is cornered by a cabinet member after a cabinet meeting and half makes a promise that he doesn't mean to keep, it usually falls to the chief of staff to walk that back.

MR. H. BAKER: Bill, let me take a try at that, if I may, to begin with. Jim Baker made that point earlier, the "Oh, by the way" phenomenon. Let me tell you, that is the biggest threat. The function of the chief of staff is to make sure that you know not only what the president may think but what the president has said. I had a minor flap with my good friend Frank Carlucci when I first got there.[6] Frank had proceeded me by a few weeks. The [John] Tower Commission had provided that the national security advisor would always have access to the president. Frank came in and said, "Oh, by the way, I'm going to go see the president at ten o'clock." I said, "Fine. I'm going with you." He said, "But the Tower Commission says I have access any time." I said, "That's right. And my manual here that I am now writing says ain't nobody going to see the president that I don't go with him." Frank bridled at that for a little while but he didn't object to it. Indeed, we worked the whole arrangement that way.

At nine o'clock in the morning, Kenny Duberstein and I would have a meeting with the president on domestic issues. At nine-thirty, Frank Carlucci and Colin Powell would come in and the four of us would remain.[7] But it was vitally important, in my view, that the chief of staff know exactly what the president was faced with, what he had said, the decisions he had made. So I think the point Jim made was vitally important. That is the only real change I made because, after that, everybody understood that the chief of staff in my time was going to be the custodian of the president's papers and his person. I don't really characterize that as a gatekeeper but they weren't going in there unless I was along or Ken Duberstein was along so that we could know exactly what had happened and the president would never be caught in the crossfire.

MR. SKINNER: I had the same arrangement with President Bush. He was quite clear on that. There were a few people that had weekly access. He had lunches with the vice president [Daniel Quayle]. He had meetings with Secretaries Cheney [of defense] and Baker [of state] on a regular basis. I wanted to make sure that I was in on those meetings so I could find out and handle the coordination. Because President Bush has a million friends and a million people talk to him, on occasion people would corner him, usually not in the White House but outside the White House, and you would then have to—he would be very, very polite in the way he responded, which would, of course, be misinterpreted by the person who had brought the message. I would then have to go and reinterpret the interpretation.

I think, though, it's important that there are big issues and there are little issues. Sometimes you can't get hung up on the little issues. If you would have probably done it anyway and it's probably something that makes good sense or at least arguably good sense, you don't want to go in and try to reverse everything. You try to protect the process because you want to save those opportunities where you're really going to go in where it's really something important, that you're not standing on process or the breakdown of process. You're standing on the policy or the principle that's annunciated.

MR. PANETTA: I think the closest comparison, especially if you're a chief of staff who comes into the middle, is it is like an officer suddenly going in and taking over a company that's been in battle for a while that's lost their officer. They're in place. They've been in place. They basically developed a certain pattern of how they get things. Let's make no mistake here, people that are in the White House, yes, they are there because of their abilities but they're also there because they've managed to be able to deal with others and to try to centralize power in their particular operation and they are also interested obviously in trying to get whatever favors they can from the president, to be present with the president, to have access to the president. That's what gives them—it's an ego trip like everything else. So, the way you're stroked in those positions is to have maximum access to the president.

Part of the problem when you go in as the chief of staff is to make sure that they understand that you're in control at that point. Particularly in the White House when I came in, I think one staff member had described the situation there as kind of a soccer game in grammar school where all the kids were going to the ball. Instead of staying in their positions, they all ran to where the ball was. Well, the ball is always in the Oval Office. So, you always had a lot of people going into the Oval Office to participate in various meetings. The president liked to have that but he also, I think, understood that he couldn't continue to run meetings that ran three and four hours when he's president of the United States and has to make other decisions.

So there were three areas that we had to focus on. Erskine was a great help in trying to develop an approach. The first was to develop an organization that created a chain of command and a very clear chain of command. It wasn't that people didn't know what their positions were but you need to have a chain of command as to who responds to whom and to make sure that there are people that oversee others and that they know that they are responsible to those individuals. So we worked together to establish, first and foremost, a chain of command with the deputy White House chiefs of staff responsible either for personnel or for issues the way we had broken it down.

Secondly, it was discipline, just to establish basic discipline, that you don't just go walking into the White House, that you in fact control access. It was very important to establish some control over access so that not everybody thought they had the freedom to simply walk into the Oval Office, that if there was going to be a presentation on issues that we would determine the time, we would determine who would be there. The same thing with flying on *Air Force One*. You don't just simply have everybody jump on the plane if the president is going somewhere. You have to decide who goes on *Air Force One* and make very controlled decisions about that. So getting that kind of control and discipline was very important.

Thirdly, it's focus. This president, at the time he came in, was interested in doing absolutely everything. Everything. Every request that came in, he wanted to do it. Every event that came in, he wanted to do it. If there were five events a day on education, on crime, on budget, he wanted to do them all. The problem was that there was no focus then to the message he was trying to deliver. So what we established was a clear focus. If you're going to do something, if you're going to use the bully pulpit, you better set a message for that day because otherwise, if you have ten messages coming out of the White House, you've lost your impact. So creating that focus, creating a scheduling process that allowed you to set up a clear sense of what the president was going to be doing, not just today or tomorrow, but over a three-month and a six-month period was extremely important to try to establish then a real focus so that the president could use the bully pulpit.

So those were some of the challenges that we had to confront.

MR. BOWLES: I would just add to that, having the opportunity to go in with Leon was a real benefit to me because, when we did go in, Leon was great at really bringing about some enormous changes to the White House and really putting in some real organization and structure and focus. I think focus is the key. When you're focused on a hundred things, you're really not focused on anything. Leon established that strong organization and that strong structure and that strong focus. He also did put in the discipline that you need in any White House in order to, I think, function in an appropriate manner. I think when people can wander in and out of the Oval Office it does mean that the president does get information out of context. Therefore, he doesn't make as good decisions and it takes longer to make decisions. When he does get the information in context, where he hears both sides of the argument at the same time, he makes better decisions in less time. So I thought Leon did truly an extraordinary job in bringing about that discipline to the White House.

When I came back to replace him, my management style was different than Leon's, just as everybody's here probably is somewhat different than their predecessor's. I didn't have the physical strength to do as many jobs as Leon could do and do them well. So I fell back on what had worked for me in both the private sector and at the SBA and later on working for Leon and that was setting up goals, objectives, and timelines and holding people accountable. I tried to make sure that the administration was focused, that if the president was saying something in New York that Bob Rubin said the exact same thing in New Orleans and Bob Reich, as hard as that was to control, said the same thing in New Hampshire so that the administration did speak with one voice.[8] I also tried to make sure there were clear channels of communication because, when there are no front doors to communicate, back doors always develop. I tried to establish good process because I think that builds up trust. Whereas I found in Washington everyone wants to be involved in policy, the process is of equal importance if not more importance.

Finally, I think the most important thing for me personally was to have been empowered by the president to speak on his behalf. When I was sent off to negotiate something with [Newt] Gingrich and [Trent] Lott, they didn't have to worry that they had to call the president to find out if I had the authority to negotiate the positions I was negotiating. I had that authority and that enabled us, I felt, to get a lot more done that we could have had I not been empowered by the president in that way.[9]

FINDING STAFF

MR. PLANTE: With the benefit of hindsight and based not so much on what you actually did but now that you've had a chance to think about it, what works best when you arrive in the middle of a White House? Do you bring your own people? Do you layer them over? Do you replace existing staff? Those seem to be key friction points any time there is a change.

MR. H. BAKER: Well, I did both. I brought in essentially all of the senior staff. In doing that, I let go some very, very good people. One of the pleasures in my life, in looking back on it, is those that I let go, as far as I know, bear no hostility toward me for doing it. They seem to recognize that at that moment a new chief of staff needed to have his own people, and I did that. I think it was absolutely essential in my case and, besides, that most of them left. I didn't get a chance to fire some of them. They just left. Be that as it may, it's an important issue.

The one thing you can't do is overlay and double that staff. If anything, you need to reduce the size of that staff, the West Wing staff, and make sure that it's responsive and it has a clear understanding of what its responsibilities are, to whom it reports and that you can have a coherent meeting at eight o'clock in the morning and get some idea of what the staff is doing and what issues are that have to be presented to the president and what the danger signals are that we have not yet recognized. You can't do that with a big group.

MR. SKINNER: I agree totally. The ideal situation would be to have your own team that the president was comfortable with and you're comfortable with. That may not always be the case. You can't just go out and replace people unless you have people who can replace them and who are going to do an equal or better job and who you're comfortable with. So I think to just wholesale say you're all out and then try to fill those slots, you better make sure you can fill them with quality people who are impact players before you take the others out. Depending on where you are in the election cycle, depending [on] where you are in the administration, that is sometimes harder to do at the end than it is at the beginning. But I think the ideal situation is for the chief of staff to have an understanding with the president that these are the key players that I want to bring in and make sure that he's comfortable with them but that those people know that you are responsible for them being there.

MR. PANETTA: Presidents are those individuals who get elected because they want everybody in the world to like them. That's why they love going out campaigning. That's why they love to shake hands. They love to be loved and that's one of the keys to why they got elected. So the worst part of any president is the ability then to say get rid of somebody and to have to support that. So, you as chief of staff have to perform that role because you basically want to make sure the president is protected in that sense but you also need to make very sure that the president supports whatever changes you're making.

Going in, in the middle of an administration, it would be very tough, even though the president would sometimes say, "I want you to clean house. I want you to get rid of this person or that person." I would say, "Mr. President, first and foremost, I've got to see the capabilities of each of these individuals." They'd been in place. Some of them had been in place for two years. I wanted to get a sense of how they really performed in their positions before making a decision whether I wanted to change them or move them around.

So what I did was I took the approach—I wanted to take about three months before I made any quick moves to basically sense who was doing what, who had good capabilities in their areas. Actually, I must say, all of them, even though some of them came off the campaign trail, developed very important skills that were very effective. But part of the problem was, again, [that] the organizational structure didn't have any kind of oversight. With oversight, a lot of these people I think really performed at maximum. So what I did was I took about three months. I established two things that were very helpful to that. One was a seven-thirty in the morning meeting with high level staff. By high level staff I mean obviously the NSC director. The Economic Council was there, so we had that director; the president's press person; the president's counsel; the two White House deputy chiefs of staff and other key individuals who participated in an early morning meeting that basically ran through what is the agenda, what are the issues. We looked at Capitol Hill. We looked at what was happening in foreign policy. We looked at every area. What that did is it gave me a sense of, again, the capabilities of each of the people involved.

Then, secondly, at eight-fifteen we ran broader staff meetings in which we brought in staff from all areas to sit around the table in the Roosevelt Room and ran through the same thing, but what helped was that they all felt a part of the process and they also contributed views at that point [that] were helpful to me in understanding. Because you have so many staff that you're dealing with, you're never quite sure who the hell is doing what. So you began to get a sense of where the responsibilities were. That helped.

Secondly, we made decisions then based on our reorganization where the changes could be made. I cleared that with the president. Even then sometimes the president said, "Oh yes, we want that change," but then he would kind of rethink it ten times.

MR. BOWLES: I'll interrupt Leon here. We had something we used to joke about we called the "godfather rule" or the "rabbi rule." And that is everybody at the White House has a godfather somewhere so you might judge their talent and decide this is the person we want to replace but sometimes they had a godfather somewhere we didn't know about and we couldn't do it.

MR. PANETTA: You had to run through those kinds of processes and ultimately I think we did it and ultimately the president would support it. But the president is somebody who obviously when he makes a decision doesn't quite make it in the sense that he's constantly looking at it to see whether it was the right thing to do. We had to constantly say you've made the decision, let's move on and look at the other decisions, the thousand decisions you have to make.

There was some layering in the sense that if there was an area of weakness in which there was somebody there but you thought it would be better to have at least somebody that you knew could oversee an area. There's some layering that goes on. So the answer to your question, Bill, is I think it's a mixed process. You don't just simply clean house. You look at capabilities. You reorganize within those capabilities. Then you do some layering mainly to protect your back as chief of staff. You have to have people around you that are very close and whose loyalties are to you.

People in the White House, clearly their loyalty is to the president but as chief of staff in terms of the operations of that office, you need to have at least some key people that protect your back. That includes the deputy chiefs of staff. I had Erskine, I had Harold Ickes, and I had Evelyn Leiberman that came into that job. All of them were loyal to me and all of them as a result were very protective and that helped a great deal.

MR. BOWLES: I would just add I think everybody here is saying the same thing, if you're going to be held accountable for doing the job the president has charged you to do, which is carrying out his agenda, then you have to have a team that you're comfortable in working with. So I felt that was one of the most critical things that I could discuss with the president before I took the job. I do think you have to be practical. You can't replace all the people that you might want to replace because some of them do have godfathers somewhere else in the administration that have gotten them in that position and in the rule of practicality you can't replace them all.

But there is a natural turnover in the White House, too. I became chief of staff in the president's fifth year in office. By that time, a lot of people are tired and are just simply ready to move on. Secondly, a lot of people are ready to be promoted and to move to higher positions within the administration. But you do have to have the ability also to ask some people to leave. In that way you can have a team there that's dedicated to carrying out the goals and objectives you've agreed to.

CONTROLLING ACCESS

MR. PLANTE: Let me ask each of you to reflect on how you dealt with outside forces, some not so outside? One that comes to mind because of comments by Jim Baker as well as Howard Baker is the NSC. The anecdotal evidence suggests that chiefs of staff often have a difficult time making the NSC report through them or work with them.

MR. H. BAKER: I need to clarify what I said. I never asked the NSC to report through me. What I did was require that the NSC keep me involved. I never tried to intervene between the president and his national security advisor. If a chief of staff is to function as a chief of staff it's important, I think it's absolutely essential, that he or she be aware of what's going on in that first, the national security side as well as the domestic side. But there's a difference there between being involved and going through the chief of staff.

I was involved, as was Ken Duberstein when he became chief of staff, as a member of the National Security Council. That really wasn't important to me because had I not been in NSC meetings; in the course of our staff conversations and conversations with the president the important matters were discussed anyway. But NSC is an extraordinary organization and extraordinarily well staffed. It has performed well, in Democratic and Republican administrations, but it has to be part of the pattern of things.

MR. PLANTE: But it's a competing power center.

MR. H. BAKER: Well, it isn't really a competing power center, Bill, or at least I never thought of it as a competing power center. I thought of it as a resource, an asset, a major player, which forms the president's points of view but I never thought of it as a competition. Maybe that's because I never tried to compete with them on their decisions. Sometimes I would disagree on a particular point and we'd thrash it out and the president would decide. Presidents always decide. He had a little card printed up that said, "Just remember, I am President and *you are not.*" It was firmly fixed in my mind.

MR. SKINNER: The national security team that President Bush had set up is obviously world class. They had waged a successful effort in Iraq and it was working well. I wanted to know what was going on and General [Brent] Scowcroft was very good about keeping me advised and I might add, because he had been in two administrations and was very knowledgeable and wise, he was a great resource for me as a new chief of staff just to go talk to because even a chief of staff needs someone to talk to once a while and get another perspective.[10]

So I think that what Howard [Baker] says is correct. Where you have that kind of relationship and it is working, you want to make sure that you know what's going on and what they're doing, particularly as it affects the president and his schedule. You may get into a debate on where he should go or not go, especially in an election year, and how much emphasis you should put on foreign policy versus non-foreign policy and whether he should go to Panama or not on the way to the Rio summit. But those issues I think, as long as you're in the queue and they're debated and you have made your point, then it is ultimately for the president to decide and you support it. But I think if you have that kind of working relationship and it's working well, you don't look at them as competition. You look at them as taking responsibilities that you don't have to worry about and doing them well so you can concentrate on things that aren't going so well. That was the philosophy and approach I had on that side of it. I think we continued until the very end to execute brilliantly.

MR. PANETTA: There are just a lot of power centers within the White House, by virtue of control over policy in particular areas. It can be in the economic area. It can be in the environmental area. It can be in the regulatory area. It can be on foreign policy. Clearly, there is a potential, a real potential in the NSC because of the concentration on foreign policy, to develop their own separate operation with the president of the United States, if the president wants that to happen. But my view is that as chief of staff you have a responsibility to the president to be a broker, to be able to advise him on politics, on policy, to give him a sense because sometimes the president, even if you put all of the National Security Council in the room, would sometimes turn to me and say, "What do you think? Do you think I'm getting the straight scoop here?" And you have to be able to advise him in those instances, you have to advise him politically. Sometimes the NSC is wrapped up in policy and what they think is right for policy but policy goes nowhere if you can't take that argument and take it up to Capitol Hill and make sure that the people in the responsible committees know what you're doing and ultimately anything you do on foreign policy will be subjected to a vote on Capitol Hill one way or the other. Even with, obviously, all of the power that a commander-in-chief has to make those kinds of decisions, ultimately they [Congress] control the power of the purse. So, you have to make sure. Being from the Congress, I felt it was extremely important, and the president respected my view on the Congress, that the arrangement we worked out was essentially this: you work policy, you work the issues. I respect that. I don't have the same expertise. The same thing was true for other areas. But when it comes to bringing those decisions to the president, I want to be there. So I participated in the NSC meetings in the basement of the White House and then when those decisions were brought to the president, I participated in those meetings.

I have to tell you, Tony Lake, who was the NSC director, and Sandy Berger, who was his deputy, were very good at working with me. As a matter of fact, if a crisis took place, they would call me and say we've got to go to the president with this. I would then set it up for the president. I didn't try to say, "Yes, No." If it's on foreign policy, I respected their judgment. We would then go in and have those meetings. So we developed a very good relationship.

In addition to that, I should tell you, these meetings that I did in the early morning the first issue we turned to was foreign policy. I'd say to Sandy or Tony coming to those meetings, what's happening on foreign policy and they would give a summary of where the potential crises were, where the issues were. We began to build a relationship that then allowed us to work very closely together in bringing those issues to the president and that's the way the president wanted it.

MR. BOWLES: I carried forward most of Leon's philosophy in that regard. I did, however, encourage Sandy Berger to feel free to communicate directly with the president but he had to feel like he had to keep me in the loop because, as Leon said, President Clinton would always turn to you when it was just the two of you in the room and ask you what you think.[11] So you have to be informed as to what goes on in the foreign policy world. Secondly, I felt an obligation to keep them in the loop as to what we were doing on the domestic side of the aisle.

I think where the competition comes in is in the bidding for the president's time. If it was up to the NSC, literally, the president would be out of the country every single day. He would. There's no foreign country too small or too large for him to visit at least twice. So I think you do compete with the NSC.

MR. PLANTE: How important was it for the chief of staff to try to control what came to the president from the departments and agencies and did you try?

MR. H. BAKER: Well, the control, of course, was the gatekeeper function. You never say this out loud and you never publish it as policy but, except for the secretary of defense and secretary of state, they all had to come through the chief of staff to set up their appointments, which was a major bruise on some egos. But, it was absolutely essential to do it that way. Once again, even in my time, when George Schultz was secretary of state and Cap Weinberger was secretary of defense, I used to sit in with them. It wasn't all together because I wanted to make sure I knew what was going to happen, but I thought I might have to referee, I might have to separate them at some point.

But the gatekeeper function extends to the cabinet level ranks as well and it is not meant to be a diminution of their importance because they are singly and together extraordinarily important. But the president only has so much time, he can only do so many things at once and somebody needs to regulate that for him.

MR. SKINNER: I totally agree. I think you have to have control of that access. You have to make sure they understand that you control the access. You have to be fair about it. And it shouldn't be absolute. There are occasions when they go in and they want something personal, you can at least know about it. They may have something personal they want to discuss with him that they don't want to discuss with you. That's legitimate but at least you want to know that they're going in to discuss a personal issue and not a policy issue. And, number two, in all likelihood, if you have the relationship with the president that the chief of staff should have, he'll tell you anyway once it's over. You may have even got an inkling of what it was all about or not. But, other than that, on all policy issues you have to control access and they've got to understand that.

You shouldn't isolate the president, though. I think it's important. It's very easy for presidents to be isolated especially when they've been around Washington a long time and they've been in other offices. They need to hear different perspectives and to have that kind of relationship on other issues. So, managing the time is key but you just want to make sure you know what's going on.

MR. PLANTE: How difficult was it?

MR. PANETTA: The thing I learned very early on is the difference in terms of power between the legislative branch and the executive branch. In the legislative branch, power is truly dispersed among all the key committee chairs and every one of them is a fiefdom to themselves. So when you're trying to negotiate on Capitol Hill you basically have to go and deal with every one of these chairs. You have to negotiate with them. You have to work with them. They can give you trouble if they don't want to support you. So if you're dealing with [Dan] Rostenkowski or you're dealing with Jack Brooks or you're dealing with whoever is the key chairman, you have to go and basically negotiate with them and give them a little and take a little.[12] You're in a constant bargaining session in terms of trying to get anything done because you really are trying to develop consensus. The great thing about being in the White House is, damn it, when the president says he wants something, *he wants it*! So, there's a central control mechanism.

When we went into the Roosevelt Room to negotiate the first economic plan, that plan was done in the Roosevelt Room with a few key players. The secretary of treasury was there. I was there presenting the details to the president. The president was there. The vice president was there. There were a few other key staff people that were part of those discussions. We decided in the Roosevelt Room the budgets for every department and we basically said to them this is your number. Now, if you did that on Capitol Hill, you'd get shot. But in the administration you did that and to the credit of every cabinet member who is coming in, obviously, for the first time, they basically accepted that. I've got to tell you, going in as chief of staff, I had the advantage of having been director of OMB.

When you're director of OMB and you're controlling the purse strings, you're dealing with every one of those cabinet members and then you're in hard negotiations and ultimately you tell them, this is what you get. Even when they would appeal to the president, we always tried to hold those appeals to a minimum. I would talk to the president and I'd say, "For God's sakes, don't nod your head just because Henry Cisneros is making a real pitch for a new housing program.[13] Don't nod your head. Just say, 'That's a good idea, we'll take it into consideration.'" And then we go into the Oval Office and, basically, decide what we were going to distribute.

I had the advantage then of, in essence, being a gatekeeper to the budget with the cabinet members. It helped me be a gatekeeper when I became chief of staff. And, to the credit of all of the cabinet secretaries, there was no one that tried to bypass that operation. If they wanted to meet with the president, they called me up and we set up the meeting. They'd tell me what it was about. So, that was really not a problem. I have to tell you, I think it was largely because I had the advantage of being director of OMB.

PERSONNEL REVISITED

MR. PLANTE: Let me interrupt for a second to say that we have a question from one of the former chiefs, which is something that we have wanted to encourage in this process.

MR. SUNUNU: I just would like to get some other feedback on something because I think it's an important point you've skirted here and it just has to be reemphasized. The president has a philosophy and a political viewpoint on policy issues that he wants brought forward. One of the big responsibilities that I felt was that we had to have the people in the White House that knew enough about those issues to make sure that what the president really wanted was included in the details because the devil is in the details. And [Richard] Darman and Roger Porter and my own involvement on the domestic side, we had to make sure that he had, because he doesn't have time to read every piece of legislation, the people in-house. Would you comment on that aspect, on the brain power aspect of the staff you bring in to make sure that the president's nuance on environmental issues, on budget issues as you talked about, on whatever the issues are, are preserved in the details of what goes in to the resident.[14]

MR. SKINNER: John, I think it is clear that the better the people you can recruit in there the better off you're going to be because you'll get another voice and another analysis of what's really going on. I think you made a very good point earlier. Recruiting the people is sometimes harder at certain times than others. But keeping them motivated and keeping them balanced for the period that they're there is extremely important. It's a burnout job. It's a burnout job in all aspects. If they're not fresh and really engaged, they're going to be of little use. There's a tendency, I think, for people to get burned. So I think not only do you have to recruit them, but you have to recycle them on a regular basis so that you get that new input in and you get fresh new people and their enthusiasm. What you get at the beginning is what you get for the entire time they're there. And it's harder as you go on in years.

MR. H. BAKER: That perhaps leads to another question, and that's a very good question, and that is how you try to utilize resources that are not only outside the administration but outside of government. That is, I really do think, a neglected resource. When I was chief of staff and on several occasions, I brought in people who were totally out of the government. Some had experience in government and some did not. We'd run them through a system and pick up a lot of new perspective not infrequently.

By the way, in that category, I might say that when we were preparing Reagan for the Moscow summit, we had all the usual presentations from within the administration, from state, from defense, from the Central Intelligence Agency, from the National Security Council, and we had a team of four others who were from the university setting. At the end, I said, "Mr. President, how would you feel if I were to ask former President Nixon to come down and brief you on arms control?" He thought for a minute and said, "I think that's a good idea." Some of you will recall that after Nixon left—one of the amazing things about Nixon to me is that his ego survived to the point where he could remain expert on many matters, particularly foreign policy and arms control. I invited him down, and he briefed President Reagan for two hours and twenty minutes without a note. That was the best presentation on that subject I ever heard. But the country is populated by experts who are outside of and largely unknown to White House apparatus. I don't know any way to formalize that but, on John Sununu's point, I think it's terribly important that chiefs of staff, the whole structure of government, legislative and executive, for that matter, keep an eye on the fact that they are not the exclusive possessors of all this. There are lots of resources out there that would be eager to help.

GATEKEEPING THE OVAL OFFICE

MR. PLANTE: Erskine Bowles, let me ask you, since I cut you off, whether you had anything to add to the discourse on the gatekeeping functions, the difficulty and desirability thereof and then on this subject, if you'd like?

MR. BOWLES: No particularly great wisdom. I do believe it's exceedingly important for a chief of staff to have the reputation for having good process that is fair so that all people believe they can have access to the president. And if they believe they can, then controlling that access becomes much, much easier. I always did, however, want to make sure I knew what someone wanted to talk to the president about before they went into the Oval Office so that the president could be properly briefed and would never be caught off guard. I thought that was a responsibility that I had.

I think in response to John's statements, I do think you have to have some real expertise in the White House that understands those issues that you're going to face on a daily basis and we tried to house those in what we called the Domestic Policy Council, the National Economic Council, and, obviously, the NSC. So you want to make sure you have that kind of expertise there that you can draw on immediately. In addition, you have to have a guy like a Gene Sperling is now, who is the keeper of the institutional memory of this president, who remembers back to the things he promised when he was a candidate in 1991 and can remember what this president really has been fighting for. There is so much turnover in the White House that you lose some of that institutional memory as time goes forward.

I would say lastly to that, I always believed that the worst thing I could do was to isolate the president so that all he heard was the little cabal within the White House. I really did want to make sure that we opened him up so that he did hear viewpoints that were different than those of ours in the White House and particularly different than mine so he would have a chance to make the best decision and not necessarily the one I might think was right.

MR. PANETTA: I think the best structure that you can establish is to try to take the kind of NSC approach and make sure you apply the same approach even on domestic policy, which means that you have a responsibility to make sure that the president is getting all of the facts about an issue, whether he likes them or whether he doesn't like them, to try to get as full a picture of what is involved. Whether he's deciding to establish a new loan program for higher education or whether he's deciding to go into Kosovo, what you want from the key staff people is a very substantive presentation as to what are the issues involved here and what would they recommend as options to the president. What you don't want is everybody kind of grinding their own political axe or getting a few people who may have their own policy agenda trying to impose that on the president.

The one thing about President Clinton was that, because he is bright and because he loves details on issues, he wanted to be the one to kind of synthesize what the different issues are and bring them to a conclusion. That's what his process was. So, what you have to do is basically feed that process. He may have his own view about a particular idea. Welfare reform is a good example. He knew that there were some issues he wanted to confront on welfare reform but it's not as if he said I want A, B, C done and then you went out and did A, B, C. No. That wasn't the way it worked. We had policy people that came in and presented a number of different options. And he wanted that. He wanted to have that kind of input.

So the real question for a chief of staff is how do you then organize that so that it doesn't take ten days to go through a briefing. What I would do is I would bring those staff people into the chief of staff's office. I would say, "What are you going to brief the president on?" They would make the presentation. If it wasn't tight, you'd try to get it so it was tighter. What I always wanted to do was to bring it down to at least three or four options. So you describe the situation, you describe what you're recommending, and then describe the options that are available to the president so the president then could weigh those different options. Sometimes he mixed and matched between the options but at least he had a very clean presentation on the issue. I found, as chief of staff, that was the best way then to try to present those kinds of issues to the president.

PARTISANSHIP AND CRISIS

MR. PLANTE: Let me ask you to synthesize your thoughts on two disparate but not unrelated issues: crisis management and the question of civility in public discourse in a time of extreme partisanship. Who would like to be the first to jump into that?

MR. H. BAKER: Well, I don't know. Let me talk about civility for a moment. It's one of my pet sermons and it has its origins in my time in the Congress. Incidentally, let me say parenthetically, my view is that the one fundamental improvement in our system of government in this country would be to increase the level of interface between the Congress and the White House. I think the distance down Pennsylvania Avenue is getting longer and longer. I think there has to be more contact not just between staff but between presidents and chairmen of committees and leaders of Congress. I think that would lead to civility. But I've preached that sermon for a long time and nobody's paid any attention so far but I do it again today.

On crisis management, you cannot invent a crisis management system when the crisis is upon you. I had a little bit of that problem when I came to the White House because I had no intention of coming to the White House. When I was on an airplane flying to Washington, I did not know that President Reagan was going to ask me to become his chief of staff. So, it was a total surprise and I was totally unprepared. We had a crisis that was foreign policy–related but it was a domestic political crisis [the Iran-Contra affair]. But, I soon found out that the only way you could resolve that crisis was based on the president's own view and judgment. I could make recommendations but finally the president has to do that. In those cases or at least in the cases I had anything to do with, we all depended as much on his intuition and instincts as we did on his briefings. This sounds perhaps unduly reverential for President Reagan for whom I have such great admiration, but his instincts were good. When some of us told him that he had to set up a different tact on Iran-Contra and he had to say some things that he didn't want to say, he bridled but only briefly and he did it. But that was the only example of crisis management that I was directly involved in, but, I must say, it was a big crisis. I was totally unprepared to deal with it but I think it came out okay.

Somebody was mentioning I guess about the approval rating of a president at 36 percent. I think Reagan's was less than 36 percent when we came there but not by my efforts or Ken Duberstein's efforts or others. By the time we left, by the time the administration was over, Reagan had reestablished his credibility with the country and he did it by managing a crisis situation in a difficult, unpleasant, and unwelcome way. That's the way he managed that crisis. It's the only one, fortunately, I've ever had to deal with.

MR. BOWLES: I would just say a couple of things. First on the crisis, I think you have to define what kind of crisis it is. If it's a policy crisis, then my effort was to try to assemble a team of thinkers and doers and people who would actually speak to the press about it from the best minds from within and outside the administration and set up a process that was as open or closed as it needed to be in order to manage that. Something like Oklahoma City would be an example of that.[15] The other kind of crisis that clearly we dealt with was the so-called scandals. I had a completely different philosophy on those. Since most of the ones that we dealt with were either legal in nature or before the Office of Independent Counsel, my goal was to isolate them in the White House counsel's office as much as possible and with as few people as possible to deal with answering the questions of the press.

I did that so that the 95 percent of the rest of us who were not involved in dealing with those particular crises could focus on the president's agenda. I felt with that approach we could manage our way through the crisis and also deliver on what the president had promised to the American people. I think that decision is still somewhat controversial but it was the appropriate way to handle those kinds of situations.

I will say on the civility side, somebody asked me if this show "West Wing" was realistic and so I decided I would watch it once. And I did. It lacked the velocity of the White House, which is really faster than the dot-com world. I thought it lacked the breadth of issues that you deal with on a daily basis where one minute you may deal with healthcare, the next minutes it's welfare reform, the next minutes it's the budget and the next minute it's Kosovo, the next minute it's Iraq; and, oh, by the way, on the side you deal with a little thing called "impeachment."

And it lacks the pain. I found that the only way that I could manage in this "gotcha" environment that you live in, in Washington, today with the extreme highs and lows was to not allow myself to *fl*oat up with the highs because the lows came too quickly thereafter. I wasn't able to keep the White House moving forward on a steady course if I allowed myself to *fl*oat up. So I think the highs and lows are pretty dramatic.

MR. PANETTA: I have said, and I think it's true, that the chief of staff's job is not so much an administrative job as a battlefield position. You have to be a battlefield commander. By that I mean you have an objective. The staff establishes with the president an objective for that day, a mission for that day. The president is going to speak on education or he's going to speak on whatever issue he's confronting. The staff is prepared to make that the objective. That's the mission to be accomplished. Then suddenly you find yourself either late the night before or early that morning taking incoming fire with all kinds of mortar fire going off and artillery fire going off on this issue or that issue or the *Washington Post* is running a story and nobody even knows what's behind it or the *Today* show has had a story that's broken. So you're constantly then dealing with that kind of incoming fire. What you can do is, if you let it go, it can panic and scatter the staff. They'll be so concerned that they lose their attention and their focus.

So, what you want to do as chief of staff is to immediately get control of that situation so that it doesn't do that. Secondly, getting the most accurate information that you can about what's going on. Whether it's a crisis or whether it's some kind of story that suddenly appeared, get the best information you can. I found it was very good to set up a team to deal with it. If it was the downing of the 747 off of Long Island, what we immediately did was we established a team made up of the proper officials plus the White House to go in and take control of it.[16] We did the same thing with regards to Oklahoma City when the bomb went off there. The problem is you're getting an awful lot of misinformation and there are a lot of rumors that circulate and the press is immediately looking to the White House to determine what actually is going on. So taking control, getting the best information that you can, establishing a team to deal with the crisis, and then providing the proper briefings, not only, of course, to the president but obviously to the press and to the public as to what's taking place. I think those are the basic elements if you want to get your hands around a crisis.

Let me just conclude by seconding what Howard Baker said about the situation here. I've been in and out of Washington over thirty years. I don't think I've seen a meaner or more partisan atmosphere than the one that exists today over that period of time. It's due to a lot of reasons and we all know what those reasons are. The problem is that if this is simply a game of survival and power as opposed to trying to do what's best for the interests of the public, then whoever is the next president of the United States is going to be confronted exactly by the same crises. We're going to be into investigations and subpoenas and personal destruction. If that is allowed to continue, then what's going to hurt—sure, there will always be the political pain it causes a president and the staff of that president and the family of that president—but the worst pain is going to be felt by the country in terms of the issues that we do have to confront for the future.

Something has got to change. I don't know what will do it but clearly it can't continue like this because White Houses cannot function when they are under constant barrage on the political front. Sure, you can deal with issues but, if you're constantly in a barrage from the political front, it is going to undermine the capability of any president to be able to run this country.

MR. SKINNER: I would just say that civility comes with mutual respect, both respect personally and respect of the various organizations. What we've seen over the last twenty years is a shift in power between the branches of government. Anybody that has served in Congress or served in the executive branch knows that. So I think the executive branch has to have an understanding that Congress has a different role or at least they have taken on a different role than they've had traditionally. We've got to respect each of those roles and we've also got to open dialogue between the groups on an ongoing basis. I think many years ago there was a lot more dialogue between members of Congress and leaders of Congress and members of the executive branch on both a personal basis as well as a professional basis. As we know, the personal relationships can then grow professionally. I think it would be a good idea if we got back to some of that in the future.

Crises. You've just got to identify it, compartmentalize it if you can, put the very best people you have on it, and then finally make a decision and go with it and then be ready to defend that decision.

AUDIENCE QUESTIONS

AUDIENCE MEMBER: We hear a lot about how over the last few years things have turned to more of a permanent campaign, both in the White House and in the Congress. I'm just wondering about the reaction of the panel as to whether governing has become more like campaigning than governing used to be? How is the inability to work better together between the White House and the Congress affecting policy making? If you had a magic wand, is there anything about what has been called the permanent campaign you would change?

MR. H. BAKER: Number one, I would not change a thing. I might tinker with it. I think one of these days we will face up to meaningful campaign finance reform. Number two, I don't think that you can do anything about public access to television, for instance. So communications, television in particular, has permanently changed the system and those of us who have been or are in politics simply have to adapt to it.

On the question of civility, however, I think that's a state of mind. I have read a lot of history. I just finished a great book about [Ulysses S.] Grant and before that David Donald's book on [Abraham] Lincoln. And, believe me, they were meaner to each other back in those days than we are today.

But it's something that has to be cultivated. I think we have to cultivate a public philosophy of decent respect for differing points of view. That's not easy and it's not quick but that's how you'll reestablish civility.

My late father-in-law was Everett Dirksen and he and Lyndon Johnson were close personal friends.[17] They fought and scratched like crazy but they also had a respect for each other and a respect for each other's ideas. I only give that as one of a thousand examples of what's gone before. But it's essential that we re-civilize politics.

MR. PANETTA: We're in a very different era now, both in terms of technology and politics and even the role of the press. To use the bully pulpit, to get support for positions a president has to get a handle on time. That's changed a great deal. We are very much into message politics—thirty-second sound bites. We're into a period when information flies across this country in milliseconds, whether it's over the Internet, whether it's over cable network. You have twenty-four-hour news shows now that are operating on a dozen different channels, because they're all competing one with another to try to get the news out there.

So, if you're president of the United States, you want to be able to present to the American people the substance of an issue. You try to get up there and confront that and immediately, if you try to present an issue, you're faced with a barrage of questions not on the issue that you're presenting but on whatever the latest scandal is or whatever the latest story is that the press is trying to get. This is no longer a situation in which the press sort of stands back and reports the news. The press has their own agenda as well that they're trying to advance. So it then becomes a competitive situation. What you try to do is to make sure that no vacuum is created in which the press can move in and do their story and have that consume the headlines.

So no matter how many bullets are coming at you, you are trying to reach above that somehow to the American people. You set up the message and you set up the platform, you set up the background, you make sure you have all the right sound bites, you try to control whatever is going out that day in part because you have this barrage of other stuff that's going on.

So, that's the nature of the presidency today. Any president who goes into that job, if they are going to get their message across to the American people, they are going to have to set up that kind of approach. I don't particularly like that because I think what tends to happen then is that the president, rather than necessarily focusing on what is the fundamental issue of the country that we've got to confront and how do we confront it and working with the Congress on a policy basis to try to find a solution, what that president is saying is "Get me the message that I've got to get out there for the next day. I don't care where the hell it's coming from. Somebody come up with an idea and we ought to get it out there." It becomes a message game. I think we've gotten a little carried away on that aspect. So how to tighten that up?

But the problem is, if the press is doing their thing, if the Congress is doing their thing on attacking you, there is no alternative but to be able to confront information on that basis. I think that's going to be the nature of what happens in the presidency for a long time to come unless the attitudes of everybody, not just the Congress but the press and the public and those involved in policy in this town, decide to change the way they operate.

MR. PATTERSON: Brad Patterson. I have a question particularly thinking of the experience, Leon, that you and Erskine went through with the president having made a promise to cut 25 percent of his White House staff. With the emphasis you've placed on the importance of governing in the White House and of vetting these issues as they come, what is the proper size of a White House staff?

MR. PANETTA: My message to a future president of the United States is never make a promise that you're going to cut the staff by a set percentage just because it's a good sound bite. I know it's popular. I think every candidate is attracted by that because they just figure that the public will respond to that. But when you set a kind of percentage as to what you're going to cut, what tends to happen is you try to reach that percentage but then you have people that are coming into the White House from other agencies and departments to try to fill the responsibilities. So you suddenly find yourself in real trouble in terms of some of the policy areas as to where to go to try to find good people.

Secondly, that is not to say that the staff of the White House cannot be streamlined. You're talking about a modern White House that is duplicating almost every department and agency in terms of staffing. There was a time when you'd sit down with the cabinet member and ask them what the hell is going on in their department. Now you sit down with the staff aide who represents the policy in that area and deal with that individual. So there are now these little power centers that are developing in the White House.

I understand why it's happening because it's proximity. These people are close to the president. The president wants to have a quick answer. He doesn't want to have to wait for the secretary of HUD [housing and urban development] or whatever to come down and talk with him. But I think it's distorting how policy should be developed. So, you can streamline it. I think there are areas that you can tighten up on the operations of the staff but I have to tell you that one of the phenomena that I think is happening these days is that we are virtually making the cabinet an irrelevant body of people out there because issues are largely being run by White House staff.

Notes

1. See Senator Baker's biography and his extensive experience in Congress in "Members of the Forum."

2. The Iran-Contra affair linked two difficult policy issues into a single scandal involving violations of congressional prohibitions on federal appropriations. "Contra" forces opposed the socialist government of Nicaragua, with the sometimes support of the United States. Despite statutory prohibitions limiting U.S. support to these rebels, the Reagan White House and particularly its National Security Council worked secretly to support them by selling arms to the renegade government of Iran, also contrary to congressional prohibitions, and then establishing a secret fund with the sale of these arms. The administration then used these secret funds to support the Contras in their struggle.

   The scandal broke in 1986 and generated a congressional investigation and a blue-ribbon presidential panel (sometimes called the "Tower Commission," headed by former senator John Tower of Texas). The Tower Commission made several recommendations, including suggestions about White House operations and the access of the national security advisor to the president. Several indictments and convictions resulted but most received a presidential pardon in 1992 by President George H. W. Bush. For more on this incident, see Jane Mayer and Doyle McManus, *Landslide: The Unmaking of the President, 1984–1988* (New York: Random House, 1988).

3. The "Normandy celebration" refers to the fiftieth anniversary of the D-Day invasion of Nazi-occupied Europe by the Allied forces during World War II.

4. Mr. Bowles transferred from SBA and prior to that assignment, he had served as Congressman Panetta's deputy White House chief of staff. See Mr. Bowles's biography in "Members of the Forum."

5. Dick Morris advised President Clinton on campaign strategy and, eventually, on the conduct of the Clinton administration. As such an advisor, Mr. Morris tended to act outside of the normal White House staff structure.

6. A career foreign service officer, Frank Carlucci became President Reagan's national security advisor in the middle of the Iran-Contra investigation, replacing the beleaguered Admiral John Poindexter (who would later be indicted and convicted in the affair). Carlucci's appointment as NSA predated Senator Baker's appointment as new chief of staff by almost three months (December 1, 1986, versus February 27, 1987).

7. Colin Powell was deputy to the national security advisor and a regular Army officer. He was later appointed chairman of the Joint Chiefs of Staff under President George H. W. Bush.

8. Robert Rubin was Clinton's secretary of the treasury and Robert Reich was Clinton's secretary of labor.

9. Newt Gingrich (R-Ga) was then Speaker of the U.S. House, and Trent Lott (R-Al), was then Majority Leader of the U.S. Senate.

10. On the "Gulf War" in Iraq, sometimes called "Operation Desert Storm," see an

earlier note. Brent Scowcroft served as national security advisor for President George H. W. Bush.

11. Under Erskine Bowles, Sandy Burger had moved into the position of national security advisor, replacing Anthony (Tony) Lake.

12. Daniel Rostenkowski (D-Il) was then chair of the House Ways and Means Committee (the tax writing committee), and Jack Brooks (D-Tx) was then chair of the House Judiciary Committee.

13. Henry Cisneros was Clinton's secretary of housing and urban development.

14. Richard Darman was director of OMB during the presidency of George H. W. Bush. Roger Porter was director of domestic policy development.

15. On April 19, 1995, militant militiamen truck-bombed the Alfred P. Murrah Federal Office Building in Oklahoma City, Oklahoma. At the time, it represented the largest terrorist attack ever to take place in America, killing some 167 people when the nine-story building collapsed.

16. Trans-World Airways, Flight 800, crashed July 17, 1996, off Long Island on its way to Paris, France. The crash killed all 220 people on board. Initially, witnesses suggested the flight had been downed by a ground-to-air missile, but the National Transportation Safety Board subsequently concluded that a freakish set of circumstances combined with some unusual design flaws in the Boeing 747 caused a spark in one of the fuel tanks.

17. Everett Dirksen (R-Il) was longtime Senate Minority Leader. See Byron Hulsey, *Everett Dirksen and His Presidents: How a Senate Giant Shaped American Politics* (Lawrence: University Press of Kansas, 2000).

CHAPTER 4

Campaigning, Routine, and Closing Out

At its simplest, every successful presidency begins with winning another term. Yet, the limits of tenure inevitably close in on an administration. These two phases—governing while campaigning and closing out an administration—are the challenges that "third generation" chiefs of staff often take on. The third discussion between former chiefs of staff covers this relatively unique set of topics. They focus primarily on the nature of governing while facing the election cycle. Can the White House continue to focus on governing when it must mount the president's reelection? Their discussion contains a classic exchange between convener and journalist Marvin Kalb, eager to draw out the contrasting pressures of governing and partisan leadership, and the former chiefs of staff insisting that no one considers the president's legacy in those final days. Policy, as Secretary Baker points out in his foreword, constitutes the *sine qua non* of a presidency. Hence, every administration begins with its desire to leave a lasting mark.

Organizing the president's reelection, the former chiefs of staff demonstrate, takes on a very similar approach, regardless of administration. The critical thing, they all note, is that the White House staff has "the body." No consideration of "good" government can get around the fact that the president must govern while campaigning, that to schedule the president's activities inevitably affects the campaign and vice versa. The White House operation must blend these two forces together. And the strategies for this blending involve close communication between the campaigns and the White House. In addition, the election cycle adds an additional responsibility to the White House chief of staff: to coordinate the partisan activities of the executive branch and the president's cabinet.

One fact divides this distinguished group of former chiefs of staff. Some of them closed out an administration that had lost its reelection while others of them closed out an administration whose second term had expired. This latter group, Kenneth Duberstein from Reagan and John Podesta from Clinton, concentrated on coordinating their president's efforts with a campaign to "stay the course" through their vice president's succession. What extraordinary challenges the chief of staff must face in making a record for the current president while boosting the prospects for the next! President Reagan, for example, recognized that without his vice president's success his own place in history would suffer. To repudiate his vice president, President Reagan thought, would become tantamount to having repudiated his own reputation.

The desire to create a lasting mark, often noble in its roots, cannot always avoid the pressures unleashed at the end of an administration. The trials of presidential pardons, this group notes, represent the most obvious tension in a presidency's final days. The pressures on the chief of staff and the entire White House for swift and not entirely organized consideration grow daily as the president's tenure diminishes. Too many voices with too many ambitions and so little time remains. External groups who want to kidnap the president's agenda and exploit any mistakes that might be made if such capture is successful concern all of the former chiefs of staff. The frenzy of the final days constitutes a special brand of crisis management, one in which the natural tendency to "wall off" the crisis in order to preserve routine may not serve the president well if the routines of orderly consideration are bypassed. These potential "oh, by the way" decisions eventually leave the president vulnerable to the crafty presentations of advocates. Walling off, in fact, may exacerbate the likelihood of poor presidential judgment.

PARTICIPANTS

Marvin Kalb (Harvard University)
James A. Baker, III (Bush)
Richard Cheney (Ford)
Kenneth Duberstein (Reagan)
John Podesta (Clinton)
Jack Watson, Jr. (Carter)

CAMPAIGNING WHILE GOVERNING

MR. KALB: It is our responsibility to talk about something that never gets into the White House—politics. We will discuss the whole idea of reelection and the closing of an administration and whether we think about politics first and foremost, whether we think about legacy, or whether we think about how you actually run a government.

So, in the issue of reelection and closing out an administration, I heard from Sam Skinner and also from Leon Panetta, a very important fact: during Republican administrations you begin morning meetings at nine A.M. and during Democratic administrations you begin at seven-thirty A.M. Now with the extra hour and a half, Leon Panetta, did you accomplish that much more? That's the issue. Why not start at ten-thirty perhaps? That might have been a better way of doing it.

Mr. Skinner did point out that President Bush believed that governance comes first and foremost within the sanctity of the White House and that reelection politics should be conducted outside the White House, that there is a way of separating the two. Jim Baker then came in to re-inject a bit of reality toward the end of that campaign.

Let's go down the line here. Is it possible in fact to keep reelection politics out of the White House and to stick to, as your job as chief of staff, the business of governance? Richard Cheney.

MR. CHENEY: No, it's not. There are certain things you don't do in the White House: you don't raise money, for example.

But you quickly get to the point, and I think Jim will bear me out on this fact: the White House is organized around the president's schedule. Once the president becomes an active candidate for office, there's virtually no way to have a total barrier. The airplane, the military support, all of that still goes with him no matter what he's doing, whether he's a candidate for office or functioning as president. The policy issues discussed and debated during a campaign have to be consistent with administration policy.

In effect, the Ford administration had some unique circumstances. We'd never run a campaign before. We got to office under weird circumstances, obviously, with the resignation of Richard Nixon. Jerry Ford had never run nationwide before. There were a lot of new things. We were the first campaign that had to operate under the new Watergate-inspired election laws and campaign finance limitations and disclosure and so forth. But, we ended up in the end running the campaign with a committee—Jim [Baker] as chairman of the campaign, Bob Teeter who was our pollster, Doug Bailey and John Deardourff who were advertising guys, myself and Stu Spencer, who was our political director—coordinating the campaign with those things we had to do as a government.

MR. WATSON: We did it very much the same way and I agree with Dick's point. There is literally no way in the real world of the White House and governing of the country and a national political campaign involving an incumbent president where you can separate the politics from the governing that the president and his administration are doing in Washington. You certainly want to have firewalls. You want to have protections against an inappropriate intrusion of the political campaign into the matters of governing. Dick mentions, certainly, an obvious one and an important one and that is anything having to do with fundraising.

In our case, I succeeded Hamilton Jordan as the White House chief of staff. President Carter wanted Hamilton to move over to the campaign. He wanted Hamilton, in the case of our administration, to be fully addressed to the campaign and he wanted me to be the chief of staff. Again, somewhat similar to what Dick said, we had daily conversations regularly scheduled in which we would discuss allocation of our resources starting with the president's time. It's necessary in an incumbent president's campaign for reelection to grant in an appropriate way campaign time on his schedule. So, that makes it absolutely necessary for this integration of planning and effort and operation to take place.

MR. KALB: Jim Baker, could you actually run a government effectively at the same time as you are trying to run an effective reelection campaign?

MR. J. BAKER: Yes, you can, Marvin, and yet you can't separate the two. It's more than just making sure you don't do fundraising in the White House. The fact of the matter is you're prohibited by law from expending federal funds actively on campaign purposes, *but your candidate is resident in the White House.* Your candidate's body is there. So, the schedule is there and the message is there. What the president does and what he says is of necessity going to be determined primarily from the White House. You must have extraordinarily good coordination. I'm not sure incumbency, frankly, is a benefit in running a presidential campaign. A lot of people like to vote against and the president is seen to be responsible, whether he is or not, for things that people don't like. But you simply have to make sure that you have good coordination because you have two entities here. You have the White House staff that's serving the president and you have his campaign staff that's serving the president.

I think I've seen this from every possible angle. In 1976, I was chairman of the President Ford Committee working very closely with Dick on the campaign. He was chief of staff of the White House. I was not the first chairman of the President Ford Committee. There had been others because there'd been a lack of coordination and an ability to work smoothly. In 1984, we essentially ran the campaign from my office in the White House. There's nothing inappropriate about that. When I say "ran the campaign," what I mean is that's where the key decisions were made. That's where the decisions were made about where the president would go and what he would say, what our electoral strategy would be. But all of the people that implemented that were paid with campaign funds through the campaign office.

In 1988 in the Bush–[Michael] Dukakis campaign, I had resigned as treasury secretary to go over and run the campaign from the campaign office and I worked very closely in that campaign with Ken Duberstein, who was President Reagan's last chief of staff. Then, of course, in 1992, I resigned as secretary of state to come back into the White House to run the Bush campaign because a law had been passed in the interim that prohibited those of us who had served in government from even having a conversation for a period of a year with people at the upper levels of the cabinet with whom we had served in an administration. So, I couldn't go over to the Bush campaign in 1992. I had to come back into the White House, if I was going to assist the president in reelection.

The answer is you can't separate the two.

MR. KALB: Ken, if you cannot separate the two and if the job of the president of the United States is such an awesome responsibility, how can you effectively run the affairs of state at the same time that you're running a major political campaign?

MR. DUBERSTEIN: In running the White House for the president, I think you have to keep several things in mind. Number one, number two, and number three, the best politics is good governing. In our case, if Ronald Reagan came back, as my friend and colleague Howard Baker said this morning, and governed well coming out of the Iran-Contra investigation, then that would be an incredible opportunity for George Herbert Walker Bush. Let me get into that in a moment.

Let me first say to all of you that it's not just being chief of staff, but what really benefited me was having three of the toughest jobs in the White House: doing congressional relations in the first term when Jim Baker was chief of staff, being deputy chief of staff under Howard Baker, and then being chief of staff. I really did used to be six foot, four inches. [laughter]

I remember going to visit with George Bush in his next-door office the day that I was appointed as chief of staff. I said to then–vice president Bush, "I am going to close out the lights with Ronald Reagan on January 20. I don't want to stay. I am not interested in staying on the White House staff or in a cabinet job. My job between now and January 20 is to help Ronald Reagan govern well. That's the best politics for you and I don't want anybody saying I am trying to curry favor or playing politics."

In that last year, we did Canada Free Trade, the precursor of NAFTA, with Jim Baker as secretary of the treasury. We did welfare reform with Pat Moynihan. We did all the appropriations bills on time and within schedule. Ronald Reagan vetoed a defense authorization bill that in fact flipped the campaign onto the national security issue, which, if memory serves me rightly, ultimately created Mike Dukakis going into the tank. He did it because he believed in SDI [Strategic Defense Initiative] and he didn't like the limits in the authorization bill. That was not playing politics even if Bill Plante in the press briefing room asked that question because certainly the impression was it was going to help George Bush. George Bush was aware of the decision but not somebody who contributed to that decision as vice president because he was out on the campaign trail.

MR. PODESTA: In the context of the way the [Bill] Clinton–[Al] Gore team worked, really pretty much from the beginning and during my tenure there in all the positions that I had, there was an advantage to having a fairly heavily integrated staff at the policy level. I was not a key campaign advisor to the vice president. I tried to make the wheels mesh, if you will. His senior White House staff—his chief of staff, his chief policy advisor—were actively integrated into my daily operations. They came to the important meetings in the morning. They participated in policy discussions. What that gave, I think, was at least an early warning signal that there was about to be a collision between whatever we were doing in support of the president, his programs and policies, and whatever he was pursuing and where the campaign was. That often ended up being more questions of timing or when an announcement was going to be made, et cetera, than it did real matters of substance because I think the campaign itself was building on the policy success that Clinton had had as president.

I brought together a group of people that included the secretary of the treasury and his deputy, the OMB [Office of Management and Budget] director and his deputy, the three policy council chairs, and the vice president's chief of staff and his chief policy advisor. That's where legislation got hammered out, questions of where we were pressing in terms of the budget got hammered out, were we going to veto a bill or sign a bill got hammered out, what work needed to be done from a policy perspective essentially got hammered out. It was kind of the place that most effectively teed up the decision for the president to make about mostly domestic policy.

There was obviously something of a parallel process going on in the national security world under Sandy Berger's leadership. Quite often on those issues where there was an intersection between economic policy and foreign policy, they would be discussed in the context of that meeting. The vice president, as I said, was well represented in that meeting. Again, if the vice president had particular equities, political equities, that needed to be brought to bear on a decision, they would get voiced and surfaced. I think that generally worked reasonably well.

I would say that it largely did not involve direct issues of the campaign other than, again, sometimes there were scheduling conflict questions that would come up. If the president wanted to make some bold move on the budget—we were in a relatively contentious arena with our friends on Capitol Hill at that point—and that interfered with something the vice president was doing and we could delay it a day, we delayed it a day. Those kinds of issues would sometimes surface in that meeting. But, for the most part, I think we focused on the substance of governing.

The fact that that meeting occurred, that his vice presidential staff was there, knew exactly what we were doing, could carry that back, it was an early warning signal for the campaign that I think kept that at a relatively even keel.

MR. KALB: Dick Cheney, in your own experience were there specific pieces of legislation, specific programs that you simply could not see through to fruition because of the requirements of the political campaign?

MR. CHENEY: Well, it wasn't so much that, Marvin, as the fact that after we took over in the depths of Watergate, the 1974 election, we got absolutely hammered in the House and Senate.[1] I remember doing a campaign swing across the country for Senate candidates. When we got all through, I think out of the ten people we campaigned for, one of them was successful. We were down at the lowest levels in terms of votes in the House and Senate after that 1974 election of any president for a long time. So, we had basically a no-new-starts policy. We had adopted a policy for the administration that said, "We're not going to have any new legislative starts, we've got a veto strategy." So we put up very little by way of new legislative stuff in that last two years because, frankly, we didn't think we'd get anything anyway. So, the no-new-starts policy really obviated the need to expect much out of the Congress.

MR. KALB: Jack Watson, the tail end of the Carter administration you were all absorbed with the hostage crisis in Iran.[2] Was there anything that you felt the requirements of the campaign stopped you from actually seeing implemented?

MR. WATSON: No. Marvin, with all due respect, there was a lot more going on in terms of problems presented to us in the last year of our administration. The Iranian hostage-taking, of course, was at the head of the list but between December of 1979 and December of 1980 the price of imported petroleum was increasing at the rate of 10 percent a month. So the economic consequences of that for us and for everything related to the economy were dire.

In addition, some of you may remember that the Mariel boat lift also took off in the spring of 1980.³ All of a sudden out of a clear blue sea, we were having 5000, 6000, 7000 illegal immigrants crossing the Florida shores a week with all of the logistical and administrative and policy and defense and security issues that were presented by such a thing. It was unprecedented really in the history of the country. So, we had that to deal with. As if that weren't enough, in September of 1979 the very esteemed Senator from Massachusetts [Edward Kennedy] decided that he would challenge an incumbent president. So, as an incumbent president, we did not have the luxury of waiting to meet our opposition in the general election campaign.

MR. KALB: But did you come up with any new legislation during this time, any new policy ideas?

MR. WATSON: Yes. Absolutely, yes. And one of the reasons that the government continued to operate and continued to operate with the full attention of the people in the administration who were charged with its execution was that what Jim and Ken and Dick and I are all talking about. There are legitimate and appropriate and workable ways in which you can conduct a national campaign and marshal 95 percent of your resources in the administration to the governance of the country. It's doable. It takes judgment. It takes common sense. It takes a keen sense of fairness and what is and is not appropriate but with those characteristics and qualities that are the very ones you want in the people who are supporting the president, you can do it. And we did it.

MR. KALB: Jim?

MR. J. BAKER: Well, I think major initiatives do tend to diminish as you're moving into a reelection cycle, there's no doubt about that, and particularly when you have a Congress of the other party. We had a Congress of the other party in 1984 and President Bush, of course, had that. You still govern. A president still performs the duty of the office. You don't just shut down because you have a reelection campaign coming. But the focus tends to shift rather significantly to the campaign.

This opens up that whole line of debate about which there's been a lot of talk at least in past years as to whether or not we ought to think in terms of a single term for president. Would it be better to elect a president and give him a term of six years or seven or five so that you could at least make the argument that whatever he does is not colored by politics, colored by the necessity of positioning for reelection? You really do slow down, particularly on major initiatives, and you put most all of your focus on getting reelected.

MR. PODESTA: It may seem Pollyanna-ish, but I'd have to answer that question, "No." I think that there was a separate dynamic at least in my tenure. A separate dynamic, which is that the House was so close, the Senate was so close. They both were within reach. The equities of the Democratic members in the Congress and the partisanship in my view began under [Newt] Gingrich, the tone of which was set by Republican leaders on Capitol Hill, by Tom DeLay and Dick Armey more than [Dennis] Hastert. That set a tone that was a separate dynamic about what we could accomplish and what we couldn't accomplish.

Obviously, we needed to have troops in order to accomplish anything and we needed to convince them that it was in their interest and what they wanted to get done had to factor into what was achievable from our perspective. We were governing with the opposition party having control of both the House and the Senate and therefore having a strategy that worked together with [Dick] Gephardt and [Tom] Daschle to achieve what we could achieve was, from my perspective, a more significant factor, quite frankly, than we can't pass this because the vice president needs to hold it out to campaign on. I think other people might have a different take on it but that is primarily what I saw as the important political dynamic on the substantive side.

I think that that tended to play out most importantly in the entitlement reform arena. But, in fact, I think the Republicans backed off—it was less of a dynamic that we couldn't engage with them as they didn't want to engage with us. Again, my perception was that was less in support of Governor [George W.] Bush at the time and more in support of their own political survival. They saw confrontation on those questions as being more in their political interests in terms of keeping control of the House and Senate. That was really the political dynamic from our perspective. Then the presidential campaign, probably from both candidates' perspective a little bit, was played off on another field.

MR. KALB: But, if you did run a campaign, if such a thing were even theoretically possible, out of the White House, wouldn't you then give more of an opportunity to governance?

MR. J. BAKER: It's not possible to do it. The president, even though he's an incumbent president, he's the leader of his political party, he is the nominee of his party for president of the United States. You must develop the message and the schedule right there in the White House because that's where the body is. So there's no way that you could conduct a campaign totally outside the White House. All of the other elements should be done outside except for the major strategizing, which is done right there in the small group internally. Yes, it takes some time away from governance but I don't think it's critical. The only way I think you can fix the system is to go to a single term, maybe a longer term.

MR. DUBERSTEIN: You can't separate them out. Listening to you talk about major initiatives in the last year or last year and a half, coming out of the depths of Iran-Contra, Howard was right. When we came back Reagan was at 37 percent in the polls but yet in those last two years, besides the legislation, it was the INF [Intermediate Nuclear Forces] treaty, it was ending of the Cold War with [Mikhail] Gorbachev, there were the summit meetings; it was opening up discussions but not negotiations with [Yasir] Arafat. It was dealing with [Manuel] Noriega. It was all of the stuff that presidencies are about. You can't separate the politics of whether or not to ratify an INF treaty in the Senate at the same time as you're moving forward on ending the Cold War. It is using the powers of the presidency like at the Berlin wall to "tear down this wall, Mr. Gorbachev." That's not politics, that's governing, but there is certainly a political element in what it conveys to the American people. Certainly, that helped the platform of George Bush.

MR. WATSON: Just one quick point. It's a piggyback on Jim's point. Keep in mind that an incumbent president has an entire administration under attack from his opponent, legitimately so. Whether you agree or disagree with the opposition, that's what they're about. That means that in marshalling the responses, the counter positions, putting out the facts, going back to Leon's eloquently spoken words earlier, framing your message and getting it out there, that involves all the members of the cabinet. It involves a lot of the people in the administration who have been responsible for their aspect of the president's policy in their area and who are the best qualified people to explain and defend what the administration has done and why. So, that's just another reason why it is literally impossible to separate policy and governance in a presidential election year from the campaign.

THE IMPORTANCE OF "LEGACY"

MR. KALB: And surely the word "legacy" comes up at this particular time because every president wants to etch his contribution into the wall of history. And that can be done in any number of different ways but certainly when you're in the White House you do command enormous attention, enormous respect, regard, and you are in a position to help write your own legacy. Is that in the mind of the chief of staff as well, to help the president with his legacy in those final months?

MR. CHENEY: Well, he clearly has priorities that he cares about whether he's been elected or he got appointed, however he got to the office, and he's been working those the whole time he's there. But I've become a great skeptic of this notion about legacy, Marvin. I hear it all the time. I read it in the press that somehow our presidents are obsessed with it. But I would say, in my own experience, that a lot of what passes for legacy is the press commentary of the moment and usually that's not very good as sort of a historic reading on the significance of an administration.

MR. KALB: The first draft of history.

MR. CHENEY: It's the first draft of history and most of the time it gets substantially altered, and it needs to be substantially altered. I would argue Jerry Ford's great legacy is the way he took over the government when he took it over in August of 1974. There was nothing he did that would or should equal the way in which he reestablished the integrity of the White House. That's his legacy. You can have all the talk you want about what happened later on in 1975 and 1976 and the tough reelection battle we had with Ronald Reagan and then Jimmy Carter, but Jerry Ford's legacy will always be what he did in those first weeks in the White House.

MR. KALB: I think not only the journalists but most historians probably would come in with a similar judgment, as well. Jack Watson, on President Carter, was he aiming toward creating and crafting his own legacy in those final months?

MR. WATSON: No. I agree with what Dick just said. The president starts creating his legacy on January 21 of his inauguration year. You can't duck. You can't hide. You can't pretend that the first year or two or three years of your administration didn't happen. You can't start doing things in the fourth year that somehow magically or artificially are building a legacy. You've been doing that the whole time.

MR. KALB: Jim Baker?

MR. J. BAKER: I couldn't agree more. You don't create a legacy by what you do in the final months of an administration when you're running for reelection. You just don't, even though people like to speculate about it. That's not the way you create legacies. Your legacy is created as a consequence of what you do during the entire course of your presidency.

There's a lot written about it, as Dick pointed out, but I really don't think that's valid. I'll just give you one good example. I was up here two or three weeks ago with a bipartisan group on permanent normal trade relations for China. We won it fairly handsomely, a big vote. I read in the paper where this is the latest addition to President Clinton's legacy. I bet President Clinton himself didn't even think that this was going to be something that people were going to cite as a major item. So, I just think it's not valid.

MR. PODESTA: I famously and reportedly banned the word "legacy" from the White House. My view is that, to use a metaphor for this, if you're looking way down the road, you're likely to trip over something that's right in front of you. I don't think that's how the White House operates; I don't think that's how we operated. I don't think that's really how Clinton thought about the world when he was there. He was a guy who, famously, came to work every day under incredible adversity often with the attitude of, "What can I get done today?" But, I think that characterized his whole tenure in public life. He was a guy who saw politics, government, as a way of changing the country, effectuating change, being on the side that people really cared about. I think that each day was precious to him and an opportunity to move in that direction. I think he thought—I know that other people have said otherwise—I think he thought that the best way he could accomplish something important was by not thinking about it but by trying to concentrate on the here and now. I know that that was my attitude in the White House and I think it's the attitude of most people. When anybody came into me and said, "This really is a legacy item," I generally threw them out of my office. I think that just was interfering with deciding what was good, what was bad, what was right, what was wrong, were we building a record of achievement. That's, at the end of the day, what really mattered.

There were certain things—to give you a more concrete, specific example: [Secretary of the Interior Bruce] Babbitt proposed the creation of the national monuments. I think Clinton had a sense of building protection for public lands that went beyond the monument question. There was a bunch of chatter, to some extent I think churned a little bit by our secretary about how this was going to be a major legacy for the president.

The president actually spoke to that one time on the north rim of the Grand Canyon, when he dedicated the national monument. A reporter asked him the question, "Are you doing this for your legacy?" And he said, "A hundred years from now when no one remembers my name, the legacy of this day will be that children will still be able to enjoy the vista that we're seeing today." And I think he really believed that. That was what his motivation. He believed in the protection of these beautiful places, these grand places. I don't know that anybody was touting up whether our director of the Forest Service is a great guy, how he was going to stack up against Gordon Pinchot or how Clinton was going to stack up against Teddy Roosevelt. He just knew that he wanted to get this done and he got it done.

MR. KALB: Ken Duberstein, when President Reagan said, "Mr. Gorbachev, tear down this wall," that would certainly be part of his legacy but it is not necessarily something crafted at the end, but is built into the policy right through the administration?

MR. DUBERSTEIN: You remind me of a story that goes to something that Jim said this morning about "Oh, by the way" decisions. On the speech draft for the Berlin wall, the State Department prior to Jim Baker objected to that line as too inflammatory to the then Soviet Union and asked us to delete it. Through the White House staffing process, it came to my desk courtesy of the NSC, which did run things past us. I went to President Reagan and said that the State Department objected to that line but "you're the president and you get to decide." Reagan with a big smile said, "Mr. Gorbachev, tear down this wall!"

MR. KALB: He liked the line.

MR. DUBERSTEIN: But it also occurs to me that I recall Reagan saying, "If Mike Dukakis wins the election, the press and the historians will write that my eight years have been repudiated, that the country is going to go in a different direction. I am going to do everything in my power to help George Bush become president. I will campaign for him wherever Jim and Vice President Bush want." But he thought that the sweep of history would be very negative about his national security buildup, the tax cuts, his agreements with Gorbachev if, in fact, the country had voted down his incumbent vice president.

MR. PODESTA: Given the debate about Gore's embracing Clinton and should he or shouldn't he have, et cetera, this may not jibe with conventional wisdom. My view was that from a policy perspective it was important to see Gore reelected to continue the policy direction of the country. I was certainly mindful of that. Where the rubber hits the road on this issue is that it becomes less about your stewardship of the economy or how much you try to end up effectuating certain kinds of executive decisions, rule makings, executive orders, et cetera and instead it ends up being about providing a platform in which you can keep doing what you think is the right policy solution while at the same time providing the maximum space for him to get his message across, especially in that period between Labor Day and the election day. If that perspective meant having all of us walk around with paper bags on our heads, then I was for having everybody walk around with a paper bag on their head with the proviso that we continue to press the policy direction that we thought was apt and appropriate for the country.

PRESSURES IN THE FINAL DAYS

MR. KALB: Switching just a bit now and getting very concrete. Dick Cheney, toward the end of any administration there are special kinds of requests or responsibilities that you have to honor and fulfill, favors perhaps asked of various politicians, from politicians to the White House, while you still have the power do this for—what are the issues that come before the chief of staff at the tail end of an administration? You know you're going to go, you still have power, what are you going to do? What are those issues?

MR. CHENEY: Well, I remember a couple that came up in the Ford years. We had a cabinet member who was particularly difficult to get along with and frequently mistreated the White House staff. He had lost his Camp David jacket and he spent the last three weeks of our presidency trying to get a new Camp David jacket, which I'm proud to say we denied him.

We had another situation. Of course, we had Nelson Rockefeller for vice president. He was an advocate of big government programs. President Ford had put him in charge of the Domestic Council. He kept churning out new policy initiatives but because of the budget situation, the legislative situation, we had a policy literally of no new starts during that last year of the administration.

They finally came forward with a big proposal on energy and it was to create something called the Energy Independence Authority. It was about a $100 billion program to provide all kinds of loans and grants and guarantees to develop energy. On the very last day of the administration, President Ford submitted that program to the Congress with a request that they pass it. Things do happen at the end to pay off old debts.

It didn't pass, but it was submitted.

MR. KALB: Jack Watson, the chief of staff's special responsibilities toward the end?

MR. WATSON: You know, it's the same set of responsibilities that the chief of staff has been exercising all along. The chief of staff is a little like a shortstop. You're cutting short the balls to keep them from getting in the outfield, that is to say all the way to the president. In the exercise of everything, you're making a lot of decisions that the president never knows about: what should flow through to him and what should not. I know that may cause some of you in the audience to pull back because there's not a one of us here, here this morning or yet to come, who believe that the chief of staff is an independent source of power. That's not what this is about. It's about performing the functions and the responsibilities of the office as a reflector of the president's power and as a monitor, a gauge of where his own personal time and own personal attention should be applied. That's the job.

So at the end of the administration you continue to do that and, yes, there are a lot of things that come in, requests for presidential pardons. I dealt with one of those in the final weeks of the administration.

MR. KALB: Do you see more of them crossing your desk?

MR. WATSON: I did. And, yes, there are some appointments, some term appointments that will survive a new president's election that people are eager to get filled.

MR. KALB: Jim Baker, give us an illustration on a day when there's only a month left on the calendar. You're at your desk, chief of staff. What are the sorts of issues that come before you that would not have come before you if you still had two more years to go?

MR. J. BAKER: Well, you hope that you're not giving a deposition or giving testimony in some investigation but there's a chance that you might be. Transition issues, I think. I spent a lot of time at the end of the Bush administration talking to some of the people coming in with the Clinton administration. You're dealing with these term appointments that Jack mentioned. You want to make sure you fill all those because there are a lot of people who loyally served the president who are entitled to something, he wants to give them something, and you have to get that done. You have to deal with the question of the presidential medals, whether it's the Presidential Medal of Freedom or the Citizen Medal. It's a time where the president looks at what people have done for his administration and rewards them. Then, as Jack mentioned, you get one heck of a lot of pleas for pardons or clemency during that period of interregnum.

MR. CHENEY: The other thing that happens here, too, Marvin, is you have to deal with what the president is going to do when he leaves office. All of a sudden, starting shortly after the election, he's beginning to think about where is he going to live, where's the library going to go, how is he going to spend his time, what's he going to do with his life now that he's no longer president, especially if you've lost the election. Now, if you're retiring at the end of eight years, that's different. But I'd say certainly the period of time for us, two items, the transition and, secondly, what's the president do as an ex-president, how is he going to spend his time.

MR. J. BAKER: We spent a lot of time too on these new ethics-in-government laws that now determine what you can and can't do after you leave government. They've gotten extraordinarily complicated. I remember we had a number of conferences and seminars, particularly with presidential appointees, having the White House counsel go through the list of the do's and don'ts because they are extraordinarily complicated.

MR. DUBERSTEIN: In the last several months, I thought most of the agencies and departments were trying to clean the kitchen sink. All the things that had been said "no" to by Jim Baker and Howard Baker, "Oh my God, we only have three months to go. Let's get this executive order done. Let's get this administrative direction going."

But my "fondest," in quotes, memory about all the pardons at the end. I'm the one who had to deal with the Ollie North situation. Howard will remember the pressure for Armand Hammer at age ninety-something. Having said "No" repeatedly on both and knowing that the president obviously was 100 percent behind what I was saying, I convinced Reagan to come to the Oval Office for a final farewell the morning of January 20. Reagan thought he would just sleep in that morning and we asked him to come to the Oval Office. The problem we had was that Marlin Fitzwater released the fact that Reagan was coming to the Oval Office the morning of the twentieth. Not only the night of the nineteenth but as I drove in my White House car on the morning of the twentieth, I literally was on the phone virtually nonstop with senators and congressmen saying, "There is still time to pardon Ollie North. You have to go to Reagan and help Armand Hammer."

I remember a still very-prominent senator. The last phone call I got in my White House car as I entered the gates was, "Will you tell Ronald Reagan to pardon Ollie North? You have four hours to go."

MR. CHENEY: Some of us thought that was a mess that should have been cleaned up in the Reagan administration. We ended up in the Bush administration having to take care of those pardons.

MR. DUBERSTEIN: You *did* pardon Armand Hammer!

MR. PODESTA: I think you have to separate [these problems] into two different bundles. We obviously crashed and burned on the pardon side. But in terms of the executive authority, the executive action, the rules that we did, whether it was protecting medical privacy or extending new pollution controls in the area of clean diesel or protecting water systems by lowering the arsenic standard, et cetera, those were issues that we thought about not in the last two months but in the last two years.

We had a very specific game plan for doing it. We knew when the president's term was over. We had priorities about what we wanted to accomplish. We knew that the president was a person who wanted to exercise the full scope of his authority, that things like those rule makings I'm describing or the designation under the Antiquities Act of park lands were actions that could be done notwithstanding a hostile Congress. We only needed to convince one third plus one of the Congress not to reverse what we were doing but we had authority. It was based in the Constitution. It was based in the statutes of the United States. He was elected to do what I think he thought was right for all the people in the country. And I think that he was fully comfortable with using that power and the authority. So I think most of the regulatory stuff that went through at the end was well planned, certainly subject to massive public comment. We had over a couple of million comments on arsenic, for example, to cite an example. Medical privacy rule was one that was well debated, well planned, put through but we were operating on a time frame where we knew we were out of there on January 20, 2001, and we operated accordingly.[4]

I think there might have been a few decisions in the environmental arena where we would have felt comfortable leaving them for the vice president. There may have been some things that the vice president would have liked to have gotten started with. But, I think for the most part almost everything was in train and would have been done before the end of the Clinton administration.

On pardons, I think the system broke down. It was sort of my feeling that we could control the system and I think it proved wrong. In that sense, I regret that. I feel like the staff in some instances didn't serve the president well. It was in the context in which I think the president was so frustrated by the system that had caused pardons and commutations to essentially dwindle to very few recommendations from a Justice Department that was very constrained, wasn't offering up many opportunities. This isn't like the last couple weeks. This goes back a year or more in which I think he reflected on the fact that he had not exercised the commutation power as much as previous presidents had. He thought that was odd. He began to say how he thought people who had done their time and had led good lives ought to be able to receive executive clemency.

At the end of the day, the classic example is Mark Rich, which I think we've established was a mistake. I can explain the decision that the president made and the pressure he was under to make it but I think permitting a system that caused so much data to try to be processed in such a short period of time was in error and I think probably the president will agree to that at this point. I think that we let him down in not seeing that at a somewhat earlier time.

MR. KALB: Did you all feel that you could make a lot of these final favor-type decisions without reference to the president? Did you have enough of his trust and access to be able to move forward without checking with him?

MR. DUBERSTEIN: On the executive orders, by and large, the president designated us to make those because he knew that so many people were trying end runs in that last month or two.

MR. CHENEY: President Ford insisted that they be staffed out and that he know what was coming up but he wanted to be personally involved in those decisions. He didn't delegate that to anyone else.

MR. KALB: President Carter?

MR. WATSON: Same.

MR. J. BAKER: Same for President Bush.

MR. DUBERSTEIN: Same.

ORGANIZING THE TRANSITION OUT

MR. KALB: If we were to spend a little time now on the transition of power. What becomes the responsibility of the chief of staff in arranging a sensible, "as little politics as possible" transition?

MR. WATSON: To answer the question, let me go back to 1976 because they are contextual events. I'll be quick about this. In the late spring, very early summer of 1976 after it became clear to those of us who had been working with Governor Carter in the Democratic primary campaign that this man, glory behold, was actually going to be president. About that time in early June I had written a series of memoranda to the governor suggesting that we do some transition planning very quietly, very low profile, but that it wouldn't be responsible for us not to do so. And I outlined how we might go about it. That's something for another time. And he said, "Yes." So, I started in the summer of 1976 to put together and direct what came to be called Carter–[Walter] Mondale Policy Planning Effort, which then moved into the transition after the election.

Just a few days after the election I was designated by President Carter as the director of the transition on his behalf and I went to the White House for the first time in my life. I was received in the chief of staff's office by Dick

Cheney and by John Marsh and others. Ron Nessen. I was received, I'm happy and proud to testify here, with incredible grace, *incredible grace,* and genuine, *genuine* determination to help us any way they could. In fact, they did. At every turn, in every way that was possible, they did.

Four years later, I am the chief of staff to the president. I was absolutely determined that the same attitude would be expressed by us to the folks for President-Elect Reagan who were coming in, Jim Baker among them. I had asked the president to write a letter to all the department heads, all the secretaries and other agency heads and so forth setting out in a very clear and simple way that he wanted them to pull together things that would be instructive and informative and helpful to the people who were coming in to take their places. And that was done and such information was delivered.

To conclude, this ten-week period, this seventy-seven-day period is a truly extraordinary event in American political life. It's the transfer of power quietly and peacefully, not always happily, from one president to another. That's the way I think it should go.

MR. KALB: Dick Cheney, pick up the first part of that story. What do you recall from that 1976 transition?

MR. CHENEY: Well, President Ford called me in to the Oval Office. He had lost his voice, you may remember, during the campaign and the last day he could barely speak. The election wasn't really resolved until the morning after. So, we were in the Oval Office. He had me get Governor Carter on the telephone for him and then he introduced me in a whisper because that's all he could say and I had to actually read the concession statement that Jerry Ford made to Jimmy Carter the morning after the election. When the call was over with, he said to me he wanted to make sure we did absolutely everything we could to ease the transition, to help the new team, to get them ready and make certain it was smooth. So what I was reflecting when Jack came into the West Wing there a few days later were the instructions I had received from the president.

It's also I think fair to say that when you get to that point, even though they beat you, there really is a very sincere desire on the part of most of the people on their way out not to bear grudges or anything but rather to do absolutely everything you can to help them get ready for what you know they're about to have to do.

MR. KALB: Weren't there any little secrets you wanted to keep for yourself so you didn't help a Democrat?

MR. CHENEY: Well . . . , no. There really is an honest-to-goodness, sincere feeling you really do want to help. You've learned a lot during your time there and you want to do your level best to get them off to a good start. I would say, at least my experience has been, that the outgoing team is at least as supportive of a smooth transition as the incoming team, sometimes even more so. I think occasionally there are people on the incoming team who say, "If you're so smart, how come we beat you? Why do we need your advice?" From our standpoint, it was a very smooth handoff from the Ford administration to the Carter administration.

MR. KALB: Jim Baker, was it smooth?

MR. J. BAKER: Very, very smooth handoff thanks to Jack and people like Alonzo McDonald and others who made our job very easy. We could not have asked for better treatment or anything more than we received when we came in there in November or early December of 1980. We tried to give the same thing back on the other side in 1992 and 1993 to the Clinton appointees when they were coming in. And it worked pretty well.

MR. KALB: Explain that to me for a moment. Why should I not believe that there is a residue of political anger and disappointment and why, if it's a different administration, should I help these people succeed?

MR. J. BAKER: Well, if you believe in good governance and you believe in what's good for the American people, then you want to see them get off to as good a start as they can.

MR. KALB: But they've beaten you!

MR. J. BAKER: Maybe it goes back to the old idea that you can disagree agreeably. We used to be able to do that in our politics. I think that's what you see reflected here in the way this power is handed off from administration to administration.

Somebody made the comment this morning, too, that sometimes it's more difficult to take over from an administration of the same party. Take 1988, for instance. We had been there for eight years in the Reagan administrations and there were an awful lot of really good public servants and really qualified people who had every right to believe that they would stay, if not in their current jobs in promoted jobs. But that's not the way it works. Some of them thought they might go from Treasury to State. Those who left government for a six-month interregnum had every reason to expect that.

But a lot of people really did feel that way and that's really not the way it works because, as everybody on this panel will tell you, it's really important that each president put his own stamp on his own policies, whether they're treasury policies, economic policies, or foreign politics, or whatever. Therefore, he needs some new blood and some new players. So, sometimes it's a little harder to transition into an administration of the same party.

MR. DUBERSTEIN: We approached 1988–89 as a friendly takeover rather than a hostile [takeover]. Jim is absolutely right, the problems are enormous because there are so many expectations among so many good people that they will just stay on in new or improved jobs. What we did was write to every Reagan appointee suggesting that if they were going to resign, they should resign to President Reagan so that we would get the letters from the president rather than President Bush.

One of the other very difficult moments or many moments is the recognition that until January 20, even if there is a president-elect, there is only one president and only one can make that decision. I remember that moment again on that morning of January 20 when Reagan came to the Oval Office for his final briefings, which did take place at nine and nine-thirty. I remember in that early morning of January 20 Reagan reaching into his wallet and offering me and Colin Powell his nuclear code card. We said, "Mr. President, you're president until twelve noon. Only one president of the United States at a time." That causes a lot of difficulties in running the government because people are trying to curry favor with those coming in, especially with a friendly takeover.

MR. PODESTA: I can only answer that question from my personal experience, which is based on the experience that I received coming in but I think it's true for most people—this is incredibly corny—it's a special privilege to be able to represent the people and work in the White House and I think people take that very seriously. We're all partisans. We're all political. I have come up with a new favorite line. I saw recently "Thirteen Days" and in the movie Bobby Kennedy says to Kenny O'Donnell, "Why did we ever do this?" And Kenny O'Donnell replies in great movie crispness, "Because we thought we could do these jobs better than the other guys." I think there's a feeling about that. There is a sense that we probably felt we could do it better than they could. But, having said that, we had a responsibility to the country to be as open as possible, to give them as much information as possible, to try to be as helpful as possible and to really hold nothing back. I received that kind of service when I went into the White House in 1993 from Jim Cicconi particularly and Phil Brady who had been Bush's staff secretaries. I always respected and admired and was thankful for that and I tried to reciprocate.

KEY PAST EXPERIENCES

MR. KALB: In a couple of minutes we're going to go to questions from the audience but I want to take advantage of the last couple of minutes here as part of this session to get a few questions in of my own that I've been thinking about as I've listened to you. Is there a particular kind of academic preparation that is better in preparing a chief of staff?

MR. DUBERSTEIN: Javelin catching.

MR. CHENEY: History.

MR. KALB: History?

MR. CHENEY: I was a political scientist, had done everything but my dissertation for Ph.D. I thought of myself as a student of politics and I quickly discovered I would have been much better off as a historian than as a political scientist in terms of actually operating in that system.

MR. KALB: Why?

MR. CHENEY: Just because so much of what you do in a White House is shaped and affected by what's gone before. There are valuable lessons to be learned in the experiences of earlier administrations that you may want to apply, when faced with similar sets of circumstances. So, I would strongly advocate that you have a good strong grounding in history.

MR. KALB: Jack Watson.

MR. WATSON: Who was the man who wrote the wonderful book about everything you need to know you learn in kindergarten? I mean no disrespect but most everything you need to know about being a good chief of staff, your mother taught you.

MR. KALB: But what particular skills? Is it to be a very good negotiator? Is it to have this sense of history? Is it to have a legal grounding that allows you to balance interests more judiciously?

MR. WATSON: It can be all of those things. None of us will encompass all of those things. For example, in my own particular background. I was in the Marine Corps. I was a young Marine officer. I did not do that as a career but, at the risk of bringing smiles to some of your faces, I learned a lot of things in the Marine Corps that I carried with me into government. The balancing of teambuilding, the crucial importance of being an enabler of men and women, a real team leader, a team builder sort of counterbalanced with command decision making, the buck does stop here.

MR. KALB: Jim Baker? Lawyer?

MR. J. BAKER: I *was* a lawyer, I *was* a history major, and I *was* a Marine. So, I've got to agree with Jack, for sure, but I don't think my history helped me a whole hell of a lot. I spent most of my history on Greece and Rome and I never took a politics course. If you really want to get scared about this government of ours, I'll tell you another secret. I never took an economics course in my life and served four years as secretary of the treasury.

But I think people skills are important, Marvin. I really do. And I believe campaign experience helps prepare you for this job, not just from the standpoint that you get close to your president that way but I think the experience of running campaigns and the fact that you can't separate politics and policy, that campaign experience is very helpful.

MR. PODESTA: I think the most important set of skills is that intersection of policy and politics and press that is uniquely about working kind of in Washington, in government. People come at it different ways. I know that Erskine Bowles believes that had he not been the SBA [Small Business Administration] chair, he couldn't have done this job as chief of staff. You can't go from a desktop in business into this job without some troubles. It is tough to come straight out of the business community into this environment. You need to have more interaction with the Hill and interaction in general politics. Now you can get that in a variety of ways. I've found it helpful to be a lawyer actually. I didn't take as much bullshit from people as I might have if I wasn't.

MR. DUBERSTEIN: I want to go back to something that was said repeatedly this morning. Understand you're staff not chief. I think that is a critical ingredient. Not having a large ego in a town of large egos, having a very good nose because things are always smelling fishy, having a bellybutton that twitches when something doesn't sound right, recognizing that the first decision may be an easy decision, but the next five forks in the decision road that flow from that first decision may all be unacceptable options; be willing to be a reality therapist. So many people come into an Oval Office, whether it's congressmen or senators, CEOs, union heads, heads of state, and in the majesty of the Oval Office get cotton in their mouths. You need to be able to tell the president that something just doesn't add up or doesn't make sense or you need to talk to X, Y, and Z.

I want to go back finally to Dick Cheney because, even though I wasn't a history major, I think an appreciation of history is something that is critical to understanding the limitations and the prerogatives of the derivative power of being a chief of staff.

MR. J. BAKER: Marvin, before we go to questions from the audience, there's one thing that I don't think has been mentioned today and that is the idea, I think at least, that you ought to be very conscious of not staying too long in this job. When President Reagan asked me to take the job after the 1980 election, it came as quite a surprise because I had, after all, run two campaigns against him, one for President Ford in 1976 and then one for Ambassador Bush in 1979 and 1980. But I knew this city, having worked in 1976 with Dick Cheney and others here in the Ford campaign and I said to President-Elect Reagan that I would be happy to take the job and I was honored but that I really thought the job was handled in two-year increments. I felt that way then. President Reagan agreed with me. He said, "Yes, two years is absolutely the right amount of time." And four years and two weeks later, I was still there! That's longer than anybody in history, I think, save two people and they both had significant legal problems. So when people ask me why in the world did you and Don Regan switch jobs, I tell them that going out to the Treasury Department is a lot better than going out to jail.

I really do think you ought not to stay too long in this job because you use your political chits up very, very quickly.

MR. KALB: And why is that?

MR. J. BAKER: Because you don't have that many political chits and there's so much coming at you with such ferocity. I think you're limited really in the job you can do for the president as you begin to expend that political capital.

MR. KALB: I just wrote a note to myself here about "ego." Can a very good, effective chief of staff have an ego?

MR. PODESTA: Well, it almost always would get you into trouble. You have to be able to have some humility in there and you have to know that you're working for somebody else and you didn't get elected. I never confused my role with the president's role.

I have a healthy regard for myself but I felt like what I was bringing to the table was a person who could organize staff to support and help. I never thought that it was more important to really support my own public stature. In fact, I'm rather shy in that regard. Maybe that's helpful.

MR. DUBERSTEIN: You have to keep your ego in check.

MR. WATSON: No one has actually quoted Clark Clifford's remark about a passion for anonymity is the first prerequisite of a good presidential aide. It was much easier in those days to do that than it is now but, nevertheless, keeping your ego in check, understanding that you are a reflector of power, that you are a derivative of the president, not the president, all of those things are crucially important to the good conduct of your office.

AUDIENCE QUESTIONS

MR. WEISS: Mark Weiss from the Wilson Center. It was already raised but I wanted to ask the panel to explore further this issue of the differences in the transition to an incumbent vice president from your own administration to the president-elect from the opposite party.

MR. CHENEY: I think going within the same party, that's the toughest, especially when the predecessor resigned under threat of impeachment. We had the problem in the Ford administration—we had to do two conflicting things simultaneously. On the one hand, we had to convince the American people that we'd gotten rid of the old crowd that had brought us Watergate and, on the other hand, we had to reassure the world that Richard Nixon's resignation did not mean we were changing foreign policy, that our commitments were good. We had to pursue continuity and change simultaneous. That's a very difficult thing to do, to get that just right.

MR. HATHAWAY: Bob Hathaway with the Wilson Center. We've heard a great deal today about the demands and the difficulties of being president, the expectations on the president. Are we approaching a time when the job as currently defined is simply too much for one individual? Is it time for us to rethink the nature of the presidency or are we pretty much stuck with what we have and that's okay?

MR. WATSON: I have a strong personal opinion to the answer to that question. It is, "Absolutely not!" It is not something we should do by committee. It is a big job, of incomprehensible complexity and power. It is ultimately a job for the person, man or woman, that the people elect to be their president. Then, it becomes the duty of that man or woman to gather around some of the very best and brightest and most decent and most competent people to help with the administration of the government. But, do I believe that it's too big a job for one person? Absolutely not.

MR. J. BAKER: I'm not sure I understand how you would cure it if you thought it was too big a job. I certainly don't think it is. I mean, you can't have a committee or you get a Politburo. The only thing I think you might be able to do—I don't advocate this, I think it would be a mistake—would be to split off the ceremonial aspects from the governmental. You could have a head of state and a chief of government. But I don't think we ought to do that. That's one of the beauties, I think, of our system versus some of the other systems.

MR. KALB: Ken?

MR. DUBERSTEIN: I agree. One person as president of the United States. The job is not too big for any one person but I do think we need to fundamentally address the lack of civility in this town, which was discussed earlier today. This "gotcha" psychology, this tear-down, negative ads, et cetera, not just for campaigns but also in the day-to-day governing I think has destroyed the fabric of how we govern. Even in the dark days of 1981, 1982 when we had so few Republicans in the House, Reagan's answer was, "I'm going to reach out and work with the Democrats because that's the only way I can win on Capitol Hill." The idea of putting bipartisan consensus together, bipartisan coalitions should be more than simply on NAFTA or China. Reaching out across party lines on both sides I think is desperately needed even in this culture of twenty-four-hour-news cycles and instant cable. Partisanship is destructive of the process. Howard remembers the days when the Senate wasn't on camera and I think you were able to work out a lot better legislation.

MR. PODESTA: No. I think President Bush has proven that. The Clinton White House dealt with military planning in Kosovo. We dealt with chasing Osama bin Laden, especially after the embassy bombings in the fight against terrorism. We dealt with the consequent management of hurricanes and earthquakes, et cetera. We dealt with national tragedy in Oklahoma City and Columbine.[5] The president has to deal with that all at the same time. I think President Bush clearly demonstrated that one man can do it and I think he's an example of somebody who on paper you would have said, "Does this guy have the capacity to do that?" He certainly demonstrated that one person can do it and he did a hell of a job.

MR. KALB: Just a variation of the question. Wasn't there deliberation at the Republican National Convention in 1980 to conceive of the presidency as the president dealing with foreign policy or domestic policy and the vice president dealing with the other and then it was shot down?

MR. CHENEY: This was the effort to negotiate Jerry Ford going on the ticket as Ronald Reagan's running mate in 1980. I participated in some of those sessions and clearly President Ford did not want to be vice president again. He hated the job when he had had it. So, when the Reagan people had approached him, he had made a number of requests in terms of his influence over budget, personnel, foreign policy, et cetera. I can remember sitting in a session with Bill Casey who later became CIA director. Bill had a list of items that in fact the Reagan people were prepared to discuss. They went a long way toward trying to accommodate President Ford and then cooler heads prevailed and they sort of backed off and President Reagan went with George Bush.

MR. WALKER: Martin Walker from the Wilson Center here. Most of you have met foreign heads of state and perhaps one or two of you have met your equivalents in foreign governments. Do you think that the job of chief of staff in the White House remains unique or does it have something in common with the kinds of jobs done in any chief executive government around the world? If so, have you ever found yourselves able to learn something, to reach out from colleagues overseas or can you really only cry on one another's shoulders in this unique job you've been sharing?

MR. WATSON: There are similarities, of course. I've had the opportunity on a couple of occasions to go into other countries to advise recently elected presidents, usually the first democratically elected president of the country, how to form a presidential staff and how it should function and how you allocate responsibilities and authorities and so forth. There's no question, sir, that there are clear and significant similarities of function and role between our chief of staff here and similar roles in other governments. But in the final analysis, I think in terms of understanding how ours works and the do's and don'ts and the watch outs of it all, it's something that is almost uniquely American.

MR. J. BAKER: As a consequence, I think, of our constitutional system which differs so much from what you see over in Europe—you take, for instance, the chief d'cabinet of some of the European leaders or the chief of staff to a British prime minister. They perform very much the same functions that a White House chief of staff would perform but they don't have a Congress. They have a Parliament and they control the Parliament. So, the functions are extraordinarily different from that standpoint.

MR. KALB: I would like to conclude with a question that grows in part out of two phrases that Jack Watson threw in, in the course of a number of answers that he provided. He was speaking about men and then he threw in the phrase "and women." I noticed that all of the chiefs of staff are men and I'm wondering what circumstances would have to be satisfied before a president would appoint a woman?

MR. CHENEY: Well, I think, first of all, there haven't been very many of us. It's not as though this is a job that's existed for two hundred years. There's not a large universe to choose from here. Secondly, most of us got there because under some set of circumstances we developed a relationship with the guy in the Oval Office and it's that relationship, personal and professional, that dictates who gets selected for the job more than it is any consideration obviously of gender or anything else. I can conceive of a situation in which we'll have some future senator or governor elected president whose chief of staff happened to be a woman in his prior job and he would bring her with him. I would not be at all surprised to see a woman in that job before we see a woman elected president.

MR. WATSON: I agree. I have the pleasure and privilege of knowing several women that would be fine White House chiefs of staff but whether or not a woman will become one is dependent on those circumstances that Dick describes. As we sit here and speak with each other, there is out there in the country someone who will be president some time whose name we do not now know and whose chief political advisor is a woman.

MR. J. BAKER: Agreed. It's going to happen. It happened at the State Department. It's going to happen in the White House.

MR. PODESTA: I could easily conceive of that happening in this (George W. Bush) administration. I don't know whether, for example, Conde Rice would want to move over and switch or whether Karen Hughes would want the job but both of them probably have the skills to do it. I think that we had very senior women in our administration operating in virtually every arena including as deputy chief of staff. A person who didn't really have that title but sort of functioned that way was Karen Traumantano who is now the president's chief of staff in New York. On the road, she functioned as Clinton's chief of staff.

MR. DUBERSTEIN: I think it's going to happen. I agree with Cheney, it's going to happen before there is a female president.

MR. WATSON: I don't know the facts here but I would ask our colleagues in the Wilson Center. I'll bet that there is a very significant percentage of chiefs of staff to members of Congress.

MR. DUBERSTEIN: In the House of Representatives, it is becoming increasingly common. In the Senate, less so, but there are many women chiefs of staff. And there have been several at cabinet agencies, so the logical next step is chief of staff at the White House.

MR. KALB: I know as a final statement that you would not ever like to acknowledge that there was a major mistake that you made as chief of staff but just for fun, it's only going out on C-SPAN and a few other networks, can you look back upon your time and acknowledge for us now a blunder? It didn't bring down the republic, clearly, but a blunder.

MR. CHENEY: Well, the "Oh, by the way" decision we've talked about previously. The one where I wished I had performed better in the Ford administration involved an issue at the Labor Department, a piece of labor legislation coming through, a labor secretary who got into see the president and got an "Oh, by the way" decision. The meeting was for one purpose and on the side he got what he thought was approval to support the legislation. The legislation passed and the president was then faced with a situation where he ended up having to veto the bill. It cost us. Not only was it an embarrassment because we got organized labor mad at us but the labor secretary resigned, an honorable thing for him to do. But it was a big mess at the time it happened and I always felt partly responsible for it because I didn't have effective enough control in that particular case to avoid the "Oh, by the way" decision.

MR. WATSON: The truth is I think—a more generic answer, Marvin. There were times when I was in the White House before I became chief of staff, as an assistant to the president and as chief of staff when I didn't speak out either because I didn't sufficiently trust my instinct or because I let another point of view on this or that subject carry the day although I sort of instinctively thought it was not the right way to go and I held my tongue. The longer I stayed, the less I did that. But one of the things you have to do in this job is trust your instinct and don't be afraid of losing your job.

MR. PODESTA: Again, I would point to our pardons review system at the end of the administration. I thought we could control it and I was wrong. I think there were close calls. They're never popular. When people put bright lights on pardons and commutations, they're rarely popular. I can go back and cite some that President Bush made at the end of his administration that would probably not stand up to scrutiny if subjected to the same scrutiny that Clinton's pardons were given, at least they certainly would be controversial. And yet, I think having said that I could defend 98 percent of them. We set a system up, we put too much steam in the pipe, and the pipe burst.

I'll take my fair share of responsibility for that. I thought I could manage it. For example, I thought the most controversial of all these, Mark Rich, given the fact that the staff thought it was a bad idea, was not likely to come up and bite us on the last day. I went off and did an interview on "Nightline" and the rest is history. I think the president managed to take the bulk of the criticism on that. I'll take my share. I'm sure Beth Noland, the White House counsel, will take her share of criticism for essentially permitting decision making to go on in a way in which the president really just didn't have the information to make an intelligent decision. It was just too jammed and we shouldn't have let that happen.

MR. J. BAKER: Well, I can think of a bunch of blunders but I'm just wondering whether or not I ought to lay them out here. I'll give you two quick ones. I was able to convince President Reagan that he should not fire Ed Rollins when Ed Rollins said Maureen Reagan was the worst candidate he had ever seen. President Reagan didn't think that was particularly funny but I wasn't sure that we ought to can somebody who was as outspoken as Rollins was for just that remark.

One other: The only time President Reagan was ever overridden by the Congress was in connection with his South Africa policy. We had a policy of "constructive engagement" toward South Africa and a lot of people were advocating sanctions as the best way to get rid of apartheid. Finally, the Congress passed a sanctions bill, which President Reagan vetoed, and the Congress overrode the veto. The president was really upset, the first time he had lost. Maybe the only time in the first term. After about ten days or two weeks a couple of us went in and said, "Mr. President, you've lost control of

South Africa policy. We think it's probably time for you to see some of the more moderate black leaders in South Africa."

Well, he was still sore for having lost the override and didn't want to do it. Whenever he wasn't happy, as Ken and Howard Baker will tell you, he'd take his glasses off and sort of throw them down on the desk. We leaned on him and leaned on him and finally he said, "Okay. Who should I see?"

We said, "We think it would be great if you got Bishop Tutu to come in."[6] He said he didn't want to do it because the Bishop had taken a few shots at him but he finally said, "Okay, we'll do that."

We get Bishop Tutu in. He comes in and he sits down in a wing chair in the Oval Office, the two of them. The press comes in and President Reagan says, "Sorry. No questions. This is a photo opportunity and I'm not going to take questions." Perfect. And they ask Bishop Tutu some questions and he starts expounding at length about how terrible President Reagan and his policies are. He goes on at quite some length and, of course, it made for a less-than-successful meeting. And I, for one, got chewed out pretty good afterwards. But that wasn't enough for the Bishop. He went out on the West Wing driveway and proceeded to trash the president even further.

So, the next day the press can't wait to get to President Reagan. They come rushing in at the first event. He's sitting there. They can't wait. They're shouting questions at him: "Mr. President, Mr. President. What about your meeting with Tutu? What about Bishop Tutu? Bishop Tutu."

And Reagan, in his inimitable way, looked down at his lap and said, "Tutu?" He said, "So-so."
[Laughter]

MR. J. BAKER: And it totally diffused the whole thing—
[Laughter]

MR. J. BAKER: —but I don't think he ever forgave us.

MR. DUBERSTEIN: I want to conclude this session on presidents' leaving center stage with an admission on a meeting that I should have stopped. As you all know, I am not a very shy person and certainly with the president, but some of his strongest, far-right conservative supporters demanded, near the end of the administration, that they have an opportunity to talk to the president because he had let them down with the Contras even though it had almost cost him his presidency.

And, into the Roosevelt Room, in spite of my soft protestations, walked Ronald Reagan. It was the only time in all my years at the White House that there was a meeting where the people when he walked in didn't stand up in deference to the presidency of the United States. And for forty-five minutes they castigated Ronald Reagan, their alleged hero, on how he had failed in fully supporting the Contras and he had given the Sandinistas the upper edge.

We left the meeting after forty-five minutes and left poor George Schultz, the secretary of state, to continue to take their barbs. We crossed to the Oval Office and President Reagan, after the Secret Service had closed the door, said very simply, "They won't be satisfied until I send 25,000 Marines to Managua and I will never do that. We never should have had that meeting." I only wish that I had been stronger in insisting that we didn't have that meeting.

Notes

1. "Watergate" encompasses a series of presidential scandals centered around an attempted burglary of the Democratic Party's National Headquarters (located in the Watergate Office Building in downtown Washington, D.C.). The burglars, it turned out, had been hired by the Committee to Reelect the President (Nixon) and were part of a broader, systematic effort to undermine the 1972 presidential election in favor of then-president Nixon. The election effort, in turn, was part of a larger effort to control political opponents by the Nixon White House, probably originating with suppressing opposition to Nixon Viet Nam War policies.

2. On November 4, 1979, militant students seized the American embassy in Tehran, Iran, in an attempt to force the United States to repatriate the deposed Shah of Iran. The standoff lasted until the militants released their hostages on Inauguration Day, 1981.

3. The Mariel boatlift began as an attempt by Cuba's government to empty their prisons by allowing boatloads of Cubans to leave Cuba en route to the United States. This policy caused a mass exodus to Florida.

4. A series of executive orders and regulations set in the last few weeks of the Clinton administration fell to the incoming George W. Bush administration. These actions, some suggested, seemed planned to embarrass the Bush administration by forcing them to make decisions on issues they would have preferred to avoid initially. Here, Mr. Podesta suggests these decisions simply resulted from the administration trying to reserve policy choices for whom they hoped would be the new president, Al Gore (their vice president), whose subsequent defeat in December of 2000 left little time for the Clinton administration to carry out decisions it had already committed itself to make.

5. For Oklahoma City, see note 15 in "Refocusing the White House." "Columbine" refers to a shooting incident involving two male students at a high school in Columbine, Colorado. The students entered the high school on April 20, 1999, and began shooting. They killed twelve students and one teacher and injured many others. They eventually killed themselves to end the incident.

6. A South African clergyman, Bishop Desmund Tutu was awarded the Nobel Peace Prize in 1984 for his efforts to end the South African government's system of apartheid (legalized segregation). In 1986, Tutu assumed responsibilities as archbishop of Cape Town and thereby titular head of the Anglican Church of South Africa. He later resigned that post to commit himself full-time to the work of the South African Reconciliation Board, a government commission to smooth the end of apartheid.

CHAPTER 5

In the Governing Community

As Secretary Baker notes in his foreword, many of the former chiefs of staff who attended the Forum came to the White House with previous experience in Washington. Some of those participating in this final discussion have played a number of roles inside each of the Constitution's governing institutions. Some, like Secretary Cheney and Congressman Panetta, have held positions on the president's cabinet and among the congressional leadership. The following discussion focuses on appreciating the White House chief of staff in the larger scheme of governing. The discussion also reflects the central fact that Washington, D.C., constitutes a specialized community, one in which the common meaning of relationships carries a particular and not entirely well-understood meaning. And where the measure of presidential power rises or falls with the special judgments of these savvy Washington observers.

The discussion begins with this topic, of the Washington vision of itself, but quickly switches to an "external" setting: how the White House projects its sense of leadership to a general public, outside of Washington, and how that projection itself becomes the message the public receives. In effect, the discussion returns to the second operational dilemma, crisis management and projection, and from that topic it extrapolates to the effect of process on decisions and "style." From a discussion of crisis, the former chiefs of staffs take up again the issue of access and the special case of the national security apparatus, which White Houses often consider outside the purview of the chief of staff.

Their discussion returns to the chief of staff's central role in the daily rhythms of governing, especially how the chief represents the president's views as negotiator with others in Washington. Representing the president and advising at the same time strains the chief of staff, the discussants note, by placing so many meetings and responsibilities on the chief's agenda. How can the chief of staff participate in the White House and run it simultaneously? What tradeoffs must the chief make to keep advice flowing to the president? How can the chief of staff get the president's message to the media without becoming the story itself? And finally, how can a White House function properly in governing when the nature of politics itself drifts towards a cacophony of voices?

PARTICIPANTS

Richard Neustadt (Harvard University)
Richard Cheney (Ford)
Leon Panetta (Clinton)
Donald Rumsfeld (Ford)
Jack Watson (Carter)

THE VIEW FROM ELSEWHERE

MR. NEUSTADT: Let me ask Leon [Panetta], you were in the House of Representatives and had some seniority of significance, and then you became OMB director. From either or both of those positions, you have had a view of the chief of staff's position that you may have changed after you got into the job. Would you mind telling us what view you had from those rather elevated distances and what changes you experienced after you got into the job?

MR. PANETTA: The view of a chief of staff really varied a great deal depending on the particular chief of staff and the role that that individual assumed with the president. For example, Jim Baker, when he was chief of staff, we were negotiating budgets. It was obvious that at the time we were sitting down to negotiate a budget he carried the full trust of the president in trying to negotiate an agreement. When we sat down we had Tom Foley in the office along with all of the leadership on both sides, including Bob Michael. We had both leaders from the Senate. You're sitting in a room and you're negotiating. As a member of the budget committee, I was in the room negotiating. You clearly had the sense that whatever deal you were able to cut that Jim Baker was carrying full credentials from the president.[1]

Other chiefs of staff, if you're not simply sitting down and dealing in a room with them, you may get a periodic call but your relationship is more with legislative liaison than it was with a particular chief of staff so that the assistant to the president who is covering congressional affairs was generally the first person you ran into. I rarely had a chief of staff give me a call. I usually had either a vice president or a president give me a call if they were really looking for my vote on a particular issue.

Now, I have to contrast that. When I became chief of staff, obviously, having my congressional experience was invaluable in terms of knowing the members and having worked with the members. Therefore, I played a larger role in dealing with the members and they spent a lot of time calling my office and dealing with them. So, it was different from that point of view.

But I think the relationship with the chief of staff very much varies with the relationship between the chief of staff and the president. If it's a relationship that's close and you know that the chief of staff carries a lot of power then you're going to spend a little more time talking to the chief of staff. If it is clear that the chief of staff is basically trying to handle a lot of the administrative functions in the White House and is not carrying the full weight in terms of lobbying in other areas with the Hill then generally you're going to be dealing with congressional liaison and others.

MR. NEUSTADT: Now, Dick Cheney, you had almost the reverse experience. You'd been in the White House, first as deputy and then as what was called staff coordinator but it was chief of staff in all but name. Then you went off to the Hill and the Defense Department. Did you change your view of the chief of staff's role as you got more important and farther away?

MR. CHENEY: I got more important and farther away. To some extent, sure. The perspective is different. When I was chief of staff during the Ford years, with respect to the Congress, we had a situation in which the president had come from the Hill as the Republican leader in the House. If anything, we had too intimate a relationship between the man in the Oval Office—everybody on the Hill thought of the president as their buddy Jerry that they used to go schmooze with on the Hill and he campaigned for them in their districts. But, they all knew him within that congressional context as a congressional leader. One of the things we had to do was reestablish some distance, if you will, between the president as president and the Oval Office and his buddies on Capitol Hill.

I must say my time in the executive branch colored my view of the relationship between the executive and legislative. When I became a congressman, I found that I was still very much taken with the notion, the preeminence, if you will, of the president and the conduct of foreign policy. I was a strong believer in executive prerogatives even as a member of Congress because of my time and experience in the executive branch.

When I got to the Defense Department, I wasn't interested in having the chief of staff very deeply involved in my activities, if I can state it in those terms.

I didn't actually have that much contact, for example, with John Sununu. The way it worked in the Bush administration, my relationships at the staff level of the White House were with Brent [Scowcroft]. Brent and I were old friends because he'd had that NSC job when I'd been the head of the staff during the Ford years. When I went back as secretary of defense thanks to Mr. Baker and Mr. Scowcroft who I think ganged up on the president and convinced him to give me the job, my relationship was with the president or directly with Brent so I rarely dealt directly with the chief of staff.

ACCESS AND THE NSC

MR. NEUSTADT: That leads directly to a question that came up earlier this morning but I think is worth returning to and considering a little more than we did this morning. That's what might be called the "NSC problem."

MR. CHENEY: We had the unique circumstance that President Ford felt correctly and very strongly at the outset that he wanted to emphasize the continuity of U.S. foreign policy. Even as the world didn't understand what had happened in the Nixon administration, the continuity was very important. Henry [Kissinger] was a brilliant secretary of state, had a great worldwide reputation at that point. So the direction, the guidance to the transition team, for example, the day President Ford was sworn in was "go look at the domestic operations at OMB, at the relations between the White House and the cabinet, but stay out of the NSC apparatus for now," which we did. Then about a year later, of course, he changed it, moved Henry over to State and put Brent [Scowcroft] in as the NSC advisor and so forth. But it was a unique kind of arrangement. What worked when I became chief of staff was a very close relationship with General Scowcroft. We relied upon each other to keep all the lines straight. He kept me informed of everything that was going on in the international arena and we worked very closely together. That was really the key point of coordination between the two of us.

MR. WATSON: My experience is so different and so much less distinguished. Honest answer, and I say what I'm about to say not meaning disrespect to folks who have gone before and who face their own devils, but the chiefs of staff that I was aware of from the outside, not from the Congress but from practicing law in Atlanta, Georgia, were Bob Haldeman and John Ehrlichman. I was an interested albeit modest student of government and the presidency and so forth before Carter so I was paying attention to their styles, to what they were doing, to the images that they were projecting. Much of what I formed in my own mind about how a chief of staff should operate was a counterpoint. It was in very large measure a counterpoint to the approach that was taken by those gentlemen, both of whom I subsequently knew and liked.

Sitting where I was sitting out in the country, there was a kind of arrogance projected. The projection to the everyman who was sitting as an interested observer was, "What an arrogant bunch that is." I must also say that even from that distance it seemed to me that there was an "us and them" mentality that had developed in that White House. A kind of barricade mentality. This is before the Watergate—it was in evidence before that time.

Then, of course, Watergate. What had been signs seen through a glass darkly of arrogance and the potential for abuse of power became manifest. It's a very slippery slope between condoning a burglary at the Watergate and egregious abuse of presidential power with the IRS [Internal Revenue Service] and the FBI and so forth.

Please understand that I say none of this as a partisan. None of it. I think that the president sets the tone. I think President Reagan set the tone for his administration. President Ford set the tone for his administration. It's been said earlier today that the role and the responsibilities of a chief of staff are very much the reflections of the president, what does a president want the chief of staff to do, what does he want him or her to be? Therefore, we must assume that the kind of chief of staff that Bob Haldeman was was the kind of chief of staff Richard Nixon wanted him to be.

CONTROLLING ACCESS

MR. NEUSTADT: I think that Mr. Nixon wanted people kept away from him as much as he could manage.

MR. WATSON: Right. A lot of presidents do that.

MR. NEUSTADT: And he wanted his own impulses checked. I think Haldeman had both duties.

MR. CHENEY: But one of the things I felt President Nixon did well was to carve out chunks of time when he could think. There were blocks of half days on the schedule. I worked in the first term in the Nixon White House at a low level. But he'd given a lot of thought to the way he wanted to function in terms of how he used his time. I always thought too—and I don't disagree with the criticism that was leveled at the staff system, but I really think Bob Haldeman deserves a lot of the credit for thinking about and designing the system that most of us ultimately used.

MR. WATSON: It would protect the president's time.

MR. CHENEY: Right. And a strong system of accountability. I don't think you can run the modern White House without the chief of staff concept much as Bob Haldeman used it and devised it.

MR. WATSON: One additional point. We've talked a lot today, all of us have talked and thought a lot today about power, about the power of the presidency and the reflected power of the chief of staff as a derivative of the president. That also immediately calls into issue the potential for abuse of that power. I would suggest respectfully that a politics of revenge and retribution is a dangerous, dangerous game that can only lead to tragedy. Coming back to the subject of this seminar, I think that the tone for the presidency is set by the person we elect and I think it's the duty of those around that president who is the source of the power and the source of the leadership to reflect in every positive way possible the proper use and application of power.

MR. NEUSTADT: I once heard Bob Haldeman say that had that burglary and its consequences been put through the staff system as designed—

MR. CHENEY: It wouldn't have happened.

MR. NEUSTADT: I think that's probably right. That was his big regret, that with the president they tried to short-circuit their own system. What Jack is suggesting is the system looked worse than it probably was in terms of what that president wanted and needed by way of time, shielding, and checking.

MR. CHENEY: I guess what I would argue is that it wasn't the system so much in the Haldeman years that created Watergate. It was President Nixon's flawed personality and perhaps a series of decisions. I think some of it you can trace back to concern over the Pentagon papers, that that started a mindset and a series of decisions, the creation of the plumbers, the effort to "protect" national security that led to a series of bad events. The best system in the world is not going to do you any good if you have flawed leadership at the top. But my point simply is that I think oftentimes Haldeman, because he was associated with that period in American history, we ignore the fact that he did give a lot of thought to how the place ought to be organized and how it ought to function.

I was once at a conference many years ago—it's the only one I ever saw Bob Haldeman attend after he left office—but he was eloquent about the problems of how you make presidential decisions, manage presidential time, and so forth.

MR. PANETTA: You asked whether we thought differently of the job once we got into it. What really amazed me was the total consuming time of the position as opposed to other jobs I had held. When you're a congressman, you're obviously working on issues but you kind of set your time and Congress adjourns on Thursday night or Friday. So, even if you're going back to your district, you're leading a little different life and you're getting the hell out of this town. When I was director of OMB, although that was more consuming than I thought the job was going to be, the reality was that you kind of could set some lines.

When you're chief of staff it is totally consuming because you're there. The president's job never stops, so your job never stops. At least for us, it was usually getting there about six-thirty even though we started staff meetings at seven-thirty for the senior staff, eight-fifteen staff meeting, met with the president at nine o'clock, nine-thirty to go over what we had found out through the staff meetings and what was coming up that day so that he was briefed. We went through the foreign policy briefings, went through the events that were scheduled late in the day. We tried to set up an office time based on the Haldeman model. The worst thing for a president is if you don't give him the time to both review papers and have a little time to think and make the phone calls that he wants to make, to talk to the people that he wants to talk to, to just block out some time so he can spend some time in the Oval Office just going through that process. So we always tried to block out as best we could a block of time usually from twelve to three in which he could have lunch and then do some of that.

Then at three we started briefings again on all kinds of issues. There were exceptions in the evening and when the campaign was going, we had meetings in the White House that sometimes went on until one o'clock that night. That was throughout the whole week. Saturday was really no different. Sundays there are always morning shows to do plus other things that we had to prepare for. So, it was a totally consuming job. I think Jim Baker is right in saying that because that job is so consuming I really do think that it ought to be limited in terms of how long a person stays there. I had the good sense to say to the president when he asked me to become chief of staff, knowing full well at least the parameters of what would be involved, I said at the time, "I'll take this job but I'll take you through the election and then I want to go back to California." In retrospect, there was a guardian angel watching over me at the time I made that statement.

MR. CHENEY: Part of the problem, Dick [Neustadt], is you don't have any time while you're there to store up any capital. Once you walk in and sit down at that desk it's all spent. Leon talks about their days. I remember I had one day off in the six months before the 1976 election, seven days a week, fourteen, sixteen hours a day. Even if you can save the president some time so he has time to sit down and pause and reflect and maybe contemplate—*you don't get it.* You're in there in the trenches every day and you do burn out fairly fast. I absolutely agree that you shouldn't stay too long. With the election cycle, most of us didn't have the opportunity to stay that long.

RECONSIDERING THE NSC

MR. NEUSTADT: Let me go back to the NSC problem I raised but didn't raise loud enough to hold your attention. Here's the president who has to think foreign and domestic all at once and he has to think political and administrative all at once. You fellows are saying that the chief of staff has to match him and the way to match him is to sit in the NSC meetings, get the papers you probably don't have time to read, and be told what the NSC director or assistant is telling the president. Do you really think that's adequate?

MR. CHENEY: From my perspective, I wasn't there as an economic expert or a foreign policy expert. I had views on a lot of issues. Lots of times I'd go in privately to the president and express those views. I always made sure he understood those were my personal views.

But my job was process. If I controlled the process then I could do my job for the president. I had to make sure he heard from all the right policy people before he made a decision. He wasn't going to sit down with me and decide necessarily what our arms control negotiating position was going to be on SALT. He'd do that with Henry [Kissinger] at State. He'd do that with Don Rumsfeld over at Defense. But to go to Vladivostock for the summit, to issue the press releases, to write the speeches, to deal with the Hill, all of that process stuff was what I was responsible for. So you had to know what was going on, you had to be aware of it. You had to allocate time and resources to dealing with what his priorities were and the NSC was a very important part of that process. In the final analysis, that was your job. It wasn't to decide what foreign policy ought to be. It was to see that foreign policy got made and articulated in an effective way.

MR. PANETTA: My view is you can't really be an effective chief of staff unless you're playing the role of being a broker on both domestic and foreign policy. Then you really ought to have two chiefs of staff, one for foreign policy and one for domestic policy.

MR. NEUSTADT: But that would mean nobody had a perspective like the president's.

MR. WATSON: Correct.

MR. CHENEY: If you had two, yes.

MR. PANETTA: That's right. And that's the reason I think that you have to keep a handle on what's going on so that you can insure that the president is getting all points of view. The most helpful thing for me and it's helpful to the president is to be able to say to the president after going through some staff meetings or for that matter even in going through some NSC meetings, "Look. This is what's going on. This is what's happening. Just understand that these are the forces that are at play here." When you walk in to the meeting, you're going to get a full display of different points of view and you're going to have to then make a decision here."

To guide that process and insure that the president then gets all of the options presented to him—have the chairman of the Joint Chiefs of Staff, have the secretary of defense, have the secretary of state, have them all there—but you're also there so you're aware of the dynamic that's going on. If you're not there, if you make the decision, "I can't attend this foreign policy stuff because I've got to go up on Capitol Hill or deal with other issues," then there will be a point in time when the president will basically call somebody else on a particular issue and you'll be out of the loop. You cannot afford, as chief of staff, to be out of that loop.

MR. CHENEY: But there's a tradeoff here. You can spend all day long in the Oval Office in meetings. Literally, you can go down there for every single thing, sit there, hear every word that's said to the president of the United States. But, if you're doing that, you're not doing your job.

You may want *somebody* in there. You may want your deputy in there. You want to make sure you have somebody in there if they're talking foreign policy or when the NSC advisor comes out, he stops in your office and says here's what we decided or here's what we're going to do, so you stay plugged in. But, you have to preside over that enterprise down there and, if you're glued to the president's side, you're not doing your job.

Jim's got a piece of paper he didn't share with us this morning. I remember when he was considering the job, coming around looking for advice, he showed up in my office on the Hill. I was a junior congressman then. He had a piece of paper that had been negotiated between himself and Ed Meese. Now Meese, a great guy, had had a long-term relationship with then-Governor, soon to be president, Reagan. Everybody expected Meese to come into the White House as the central figure. Jim said he's the new kid on the block, the outsider just coming in. So, Jim had laid down on one side of the piece of paper things like personnel, process, schedule, speech writing, legislative relations. That was his side of the chart. On the other side of the chart were all the policy areas that Ed Meese was responsible for.

I wanted Jim's side of that ledger! He knew exactly what he was doing when he went in and he was an effective chief of staff, because those were the items that he had that let him control and preside over the White House. You could have all the policy debates you wanted but, if you didn't control the speech writing process, you weren't going to be effective. Everybody thinks you make policy decisions and then you write a speech to announce a policy. It doesn't work that way. You schedule the speech and that's what forces the policy decisions to get made, the speech drives policy instead of the other way around.

MR. WATSON: I absolutely agree.

THE WHITE HOUSE WORK DAY

MR. NEUSTADT: Now, I sense a difference between you two, Leon [Panetta] and Dick [Cheney]. On this foreign policy politics side, Leon was saying you have to be in the room to hear the NSC assistant's advice to the president and you have to sit through some NSC meetings to get the background so you understand the subtleties. And, Dick, you were saying is you haven't got time to sit through all of the things the president sits through. You have to do it by shorthand. You have to be sure the NSC assistant will brief you before or after.

MR. PANETTA: Obviously there are lots of meetings and there are lots of policy sessions. You can't be at all of them and you need somebody to cover for you at a lot of those. But when it comes to the decision-making process and when it involves the president or the presentation to the president, then you need to be in that room.

MR. CHENEY: It's not an "either/or" proposition, though, Dick [Neustadt].

You don't attend all the meetings or not attend any of the meetings. An NSC meeting where you're getting ready for a summit, you're probably going to spend some time in that meeting. You're managing a crisis, you have to evacuate the embassy in Beirut, you're in that meeting! But there are regular, routine sessions where you don't. I found I didn't have the time to go to all those meetings and I had to trust others like Brent Scowcroft, frankly, who was a genius at it and has done the job twice. That was the key relationship for me.

Then I'd go in at the end of the day and go over everything we'd done that day with the president and lots of times if he had things he was working in the international arena he'd want to make sure I was aware of, we'd share back and forth. So, I always felt that I stayed adequately involved without having to attend every single meeting.

CONNECTING WITH THE PRESS

MR. NEUSTADT: Let me turn to something quite different. Dick Cheney, in your time as I understand it, the three national networks were said in polls to be the primary news source for 80 percent of the American public. In 1996 that same figure was down to 50 percent and sliding. In 1996 and thereafter, there were a hundred-and-some-odd television channels. According to polls again, the public was getting their news from the wide range across them.

Two questions that I'd like your views on: Short of the crisis that gets on all hundred channels somehow, is there still a national public or has it been chopped up among these news sources? And if there is a national public any more, or if it can be created, how does the president get his hands on it?

MR. CHENEY: When I took over the corner office there in the West Wing, there were four TV sets in there, a bank of three small ones and then a bigger one. This was 1975. I could literally sit there—this was a rig that had been put in place by Bob Haldeman when he had the office. I think it was still there when Jack [Watson] moved in.

MR. WATSON: It was.

MR. CHENEY: I could sit there with my remote control and watch all three network news shows at one time and see nearly all of the electronic, certainly the video, political news that was going on worldwide, outside of the United States. You couldn't do that today. Can you imagine a hundred TV sets up there so you could watch CNN and CNN*fn* and CNBC and all of them simultaneously?

So we were governed very much by the dynamic of trying to manage our image, the message we were trying to put out but the networks carried a very big stick. They were crucial in terms of whether or not you could get on the air with a presidential address to the nation. They were key in terms of campaign. They were going to be front and center in any presidential debate. I think they played a more prominent role than they do today. Today, we do have a multiplicity of sources and I think from Leon's standpoint it was probably tougher to manage those hundred channels than it was for us to do the three, although we didn't always get as good a result as we hoped.

MR. PANETTA: When I became chief of staff, I wanted to go down to the Situation Room to see what it was like, to see if it looked like that scene from *Dr. Strangelove*. It's obviously a much smaller room but I also thought it was the center of all information that came in from the world, our agencies and satellites all of that, that it flowed into the Situation Room. I asked where the center of information was and they said, "It's over here in the corner." They brought me over there and there were two guys in uniform watching CNN news at the time. I said, "Holy cow, this is our communications to the world!" During the Persian Gulf, obviously, CNN played a large role.

MR. CHENEY: Right.

MR. PANETTA: I think what's happened now is because of this tremendous diversification of information going out on so many different levels with different news shows, different cable networks, the Internet, constant news that's going out and the competition and the money that's involved in that competition, that it's very difficult for a president to grab hold of all of that and say, "Wait a minute, I want to give an address to the country on an issue." It was interesting to me when they were thinking about talking to the country on the China trade issue that some of the networks said, "No, no, you can't disrupt our primetime programs." The president would have to do a cameo on *The West Wing* in order to talk to the public. It had gotten down to that.

So the question then becomes, how does the president get the message across unless you're trying to get on every one of those operations? Whether it's China trade or what have you, what the White House tries to do now is to make sure that the message goes out on each of these various levels. You have cabinet secretaries who are out there talking to cable operations, different news networks, same message. The president is appearing on different shows, the *Today* show, et cetera, get his message out. Then he appears with Tom Brokaw or any of the nightly anchors to try to get the message out that way. So you're trying then to hit all of these operations because the press itself will not allow the president in one moment to say to the nation, "Excuse me, we've got a big issue and this is what I'd like to do about it."

If there were a major crisis, I'm sure they would allow that time. But if the president is going to use the bully pulpit then the president is going to have to learn to work with this tremendous revolution that's going on in information and to compete with that. The most competitive news of all for a president will be not substantive news but scandalous news of any kind. That's why if the Congress decides to investigate this member or that member or this cabinet official or that official then that becomes major news on MSNBC, CNBC. So you're always competing, then, in terms of substance versus this kind of news. I think it's going to be a big challenge for future presidents. I don't know how they get a handle on that without kind of standing on their head then and becoming entertainment. If politics becomes total entertainment, then you're really going to lose the president's ability to be a statesman in the job. They're going to be showmen, not statesmen.

MR. WATSON: Only two quick additional points. One is that historically and now more than ever before presidents and their people have to target their audiences. You don't want to go out on the national stage all the time.

Let me give you an example. When President Carter decided that he was going to do a Panama Canal treaty—every president since Eisenhower had talked about the imperative of negotiating a treaty with the Republic of Panama, in effect, transferring power over the Canal back to them.[2] It required so much political capital that nobody had ever done it. President Carter decided to do it. He had a 19 percent approval rating. There were very significant voices of opposition to that within our own party and from the Republican Party leaders. So what we started to do was we knew where we needed votes, we knew what senators were in what districts, we knew [who] were the chief opinion-makers in those places, and we started a whole series of briefings bringing in the editors of the Charlotte newspaper and so forth. Mississippi. Louisiana. Texas. We were targeting our message both by personal briefings of those who would then in turn be briefing others, hundreds and thousands of people.

Now, Dick [Neustadt], interestingly, although there are many disadvantages to the current situation, the advantage is when you didn't have something that rose to the level of a national big one-time issue, scandal or otherwise, the bar to get on was set so high. Now you have hundreds of choices of how you can use all these other channels, these other mediums of communication, cable and otherwise, to get out there.

Second point. We haven't mentioned the Internet but let me just say without any explanation necessary for this audience I'm sure, that perhaps the greatest information revolution in terms of dissemination is the Internet. The effective political and governance use of that incredibly powerful and incredibly dangerous medium of information transfer is one of the great challenges we've got.

MR. CHENEY: I'd mention just one other point too on this, Dick [Neustadt], and Leon [Panetta] probably would be a better one to address it than I am. We tend to look at the effect of these hundred channels now within the context of scandal because, of course, of what we've been through with the Clinton administration. I'm not sure that's a fair way to judge what the long-term consequences are. I'm not sure how they're going to function when you have an administration that didn't have that kind of controversy. It may be that the overall level of attention goes down but the amount of information that goes to those few people as a society that are actively, politically engaged is of a higher quality than before.

MR. NEUSTADT: And inside the Beltway becomes the chief source of politics?

MR. WATSON: One little known fact is that members of Congress in both the House and the Senate regularly produce video and television programs that are going only back to their districts or their states. One very effective way both to build friends and alliances and to get information out that you want to get out is to agree to cooperate with those members of Congress by sending somebody in the know on a subject that is of interest and relevance to them and their district or their constituency up to the Hill to sit down for their half-hour show. It's modest, it's small but, over time, it's effective.

MR. NEUSTADT: Well, let me ask you one more thing. I read a couple of memoirs that made me aware as I hadn't been that in the fall of 1995 the Clinton administration had raised the funds to buy time for television ads all across the country but not where the floor plugs are, not in New York, Washington, or L.A. They weren't anxious for the print media to notice. Now these ads were supposed to improve the atmosphere for the president in case Newt Gingrich forced the closure of the government.[3] Is that a harbinger of the future?

MR. PANETTA: If the Congress will not face campaign reform, you're going to have a situation in which what presidents will do is they will establish soft money funds even if they decide to use the party funds or use other elements. Candidates right now have both a soft money fund as well as the regular hard money fund and they're running ads with both of those to compete against their opponents. So you have a situation now where both sides feel that the most important thing is to raise both a great deal of hard money and a great deal of soft money to be able to do that.

Now, to your question, President Clinton came into office feeling that one of the things he was successful in doing was the town hall meeting format. The president got that down and was very successful at it and, obviously, President Bush was not as effective at using that kind of vehicle. President Clinton felt a combination of that plus getting on various news sources that were developing that he was on the cutting edge of getting ahead in the message game.

What happened then were two things that I think impacted on his judgment. Number one was healthcare reform.[4] In healthcare reform he saw a tremendous amount of money that was raised in opposition to healthcare reform with a number of very effective ads that literally cut the legs out from under reform. Now there were other problems, obviously, with the issue. But he always felt that the problem with healthcare reform was that a tremendous amount of money had been raised by the opponents to undercut it through the use of those ads.

The second thing was the election in 1994 where the Republicans took over the Congress and he felt that they had been very effective at being able to use attack ads on various issues to go after the Democrats in the Congress. Soon after that he decided, "That is not going to happen to me again!" As a result of that decision, he felt that to reestablish his leverage and be able to move issues and be able to negotiate that he would have to do the kinds of things that he did. It's a question of how do you impact on people's judgments.

AUDIENCE QUESTIONS

MR. KESSEL: John Kessel, Ohio State University. This morning as well as this afternoon, you and your colleagues have said that you have to spend a lot of your personal time on the Hill, you have to spend time with the press. In this hour you've talked about National Security Council, foreign policy, on top of which you also have to spend time staying on top of economics. There's also domestic policy. My question is, how do you strike a balance between intervention in particular substantive areas and still maintaining your overall responsibility?

MR. PANETTA: That's why you should only stay in the job a short period of time. You obviously have to use good judgment. You were probably brought into the job because of your judgment to begin with but you better damn well use good judgment with regards to how you then disperse your time within the job itself. You have to organize it so that you aren't spread all over the place. Frankly, if you're running frantically around covering all of these bases, you're not much good to the president of the United States. You have to make sure that you're prioritizing your time to cover the most important issues with the president's blessing.

I had the advantage of having been in the Congress before I came there. That was an advantage in terms of dealing with the Congress so that when I would go up and deal with the leadership and cover legislation up there, that was the time I was prioritizing with the president's blessing because what happened is leadership knew that if they dealt with me they were dealing with the president in trying to get things done. Secondly, my budget experience was also extremely helpful in obviously negotiating on budget issues. So I focused on those things where I could be helpful to the president.

But you have to prioritize your time. You can't be at all meetings. You can't cover all bases. You can't be at all events. What you have to do is to be able to delegate those responsibilities within the operation to your deputies and to the policy people that are part of the White House. Trust is important between the president and the chief of staff. Let me tell you, trust is equally important between the chief of staff and those who are staff members under that person's authority. He's got to be able to trust people that they can go up and cover some of these bases and then report back to him so that he knows what's going on. So delegation of authority is the way in part you prioritize your responsibilities.

MR. CHENEY: One other thing I'd add: it helps a lot to have a principal, a president, with a well-defined philosophy, a sense of who he is and what he believes. Then it's relatively easy if you're a cabinet member or the chief of staff to go out and represent him and to make decisions within the context of an intellectual framework and be fairly confident you're going to get it right. If, on the other hand, you have somebody who doesn't have deep convictions or doesn't have a deep philosophy or his views change all the time, you're not certain what you're looking at over your shoulder and you can find yourself getting out on an issue and having the rug pulled out from under you because he changed his mind at the last minute. So it makes a lot of difference, I think, who the boss is and what kind of overall guidance you have from him.

MR. WATSON: I'll just add one point. One of the things in addition to the delegation that is necessary for the very reasons embodied in your question, the White House chief of staff cannot do everybody's job. In addition to the delegation, you have to be careful not to devalue the coin of the realm of all of your key staff people. People really need to understand on the Hill, in our case, that when Stu Eisenstat is up there speaking, negotiating, conferring with members of Congress and the committees and so forth, that he's up there on a policy matter representing the president. The White House chief of staff doesn't need to be there. One of the reasons that Leon did more of that I think than most of us did was because of his long-standing and respected congressional experience. A very different situation.

It's very important for the chief of staff to enable the president's people to do their jobs and not get in the way. Ultimately, the White House chief of staff is there when problems develop, when breakdowns start occurring, making sure that the process itself is working properly and that the information flows in and among all the people who need to be representing the president's policy view. That's the White House chief of staff's role.

Notes

1. Thomas Foley (D-Wa) was then-Speaker of the U.S. House, and Robert Michael (R-Il) was then–House Minority Leader.

2. President Carter successfully shepherded a Senate confirmation of a treaty ending American control of the Panama Canal, which had been negotiated by the Nixon-Ford administrations.

3. In what became a masterstroke of political strategy, President Clinton (at the time suffering mightily in the public polls) maneuvered the then-Republican majority in Congress to hold out for their own budget priorities even though to do so caused the national government to shut down operations twice during a short period of time. As suggested by Professor Neustadt, the public placed the entire blame for the shutdown on the Republican congressional leadership and President Clinton's popular approval soared. Later, Speaker Gingrich summed up his frustrations with Clinton's maneuvering by saying that during the budget struggle he felt like "a Triple A ball player who can't hit major league pitching." See Richard Fenno, Jr., *Learning to Govern: An Institutional View of the 104th Congress* (Washington, D.C: Brookings Institution Press, 1997).

4. A major campaign pledge of Bill Clinton was that his administration would champion reform of the American system of healthcare provision and funding. Through a presidential commission chaired by his wife, Hilary Clinton, the president amassed a sizable reform package in mid-1993. The president conveyed his plan to the Congress in a nationally televised address before a joint session of Congress in which he dramatically promised to veto any legislation that did not contain principle elements of his plan. Opponents mounted a massive television campaign against the proposal and it stalled in Congress and eventually was abandoned by the administration. See Bob Woodward, *The Agenda: Inside the Clinton White House* (New York: Simon and Schuster, 1994) or Barbara Sinclair's assessment of reform in her 1996 article "Trying to Govern Positively in a Negative Era: Clinton and the 103rd Congress," in *The Clinton Presidency: First Appraisals,* ed. Colin Campbell and Bert A. Rockman (Chatham, N.J.: Chatham House Publishers), pp. 88–125.

Assessing Transition 2001

An Epilogue by Terry Sullivan

Lessons that are so obvious in this town are never learned and every-
body has to reinvent the wheel.
—Leon Panetta, "Running the White House"
Heritage Foundation symposium, November 18, 1999

Only one person has ever repeated as White House chief of staff. Given this
simple historical fact and the propensity of a new president's team to arrive in
town bearing the triple curses of arrogance, adrenalin, and naiveté, managing
to govern can easily become a matter of on-the-job training. Assuring the
smooth transfer of authority in spite of these probabilities prompted the former
White House chiefs of staff to convene. They wanted to make a public record
of those lessons they knew would make the job easier. At the Forum, they did
not know who would receive their advice. As it turned out, several of the former
chiefs who participated would play a prominent role in the transition and new
government of George W. Bush. That particular day in June of 2000, however, they only wanted to make the new chief's transition as smooth and as
effective as they could.

The mystery disappeared the morning of November 2, 2000, when Andrew H. Card, Jr., went to work knowing that in a very few weeks he would
likely lead a team into the nerve center as the chief of staff.[1] Though he did
not know who would join him, Secretary Card worked with several advantages that day. First, he had a head start, and with that head start, one objective of the Baker Institute convocation of former chiefs of staff had been

met—to lay the foundation for early planning *during* the presidential campaign. Though the next few weeks would present an extraordinary tableau of political crisis, behind those scenes Card's White House transition progressed, methodically incorporating the lessons other chiefs of staff had offered.

Andrew Card had two other advantages that first morning. First, he had his own experiences, including positions both inside and outside of the White House. From the outside, he had served as political operative for candidate George H. W. Bush, as a member of President Bush's cabinet, and then as a private lobbyist for General Motors. From the inside, no one else possessed more experience working in the White House. Hired originally by James A. Baker, III, during the Reagan "troika," Card had worked, by his count, with eight White House chiefs of staff.[2] Thus, he possessed an extraordinarily learned view on the nature and demands of White House operations.[3]

Second, Card had George W. Bush. The former chiefs of staff had convened in Washington to invest their substantial and collective reputations in publicly underscoring the respectability of and need for early planning. By their collective appearance, they hoped the country would understand that it no longer could afford presidential candidates, or media, or voters who thought such planning presumptuous. Beginning in the spring of 1999, Governor Bush reorganized his staff, moving his then–chief of staff Joe Albaugh into the campaign as director and Clay Johnson III from appointments director to chief of staff. Governor Bush then charged Johnson to "develop a plan for what we should do after we win." A year later, with the primary season behind him and the prospects of the general campaign settling in, candidate Bush worried about their planning effort finding its way into the campaign coverage. Having thought through this problem for almost a year, Johnson responded by stressing the necessity of the task. "It has to happen," he recalls telling the governor, "We just have to figure out the best way to spin it. It's irresponsible not to be doing this." Persuaded and committed to his earlier decision, candidate Bush took Johnson's advice. Thus, the former chiefs of staff reached a second of their goals when, only a few days after the Forum and bolstered by Johnson's own argument, the Bush for President senior campaign staff approved Clay Johnson's program, setting out eight goals for their presidential transition still five months in the future, *if* at all.[4]

This essay assesses the 2001 transition to the George W. Bush White House. It identifies six transition goals organized around the two operational dilemmas introduced earlier. Using materials from interviews with the principals and corroborating analysis, it evaluates how well the Bush White House organized itself to realize these goals. It concludes that on balance, the 2001 transition set records, clearly besting previous transitions despite the obvious challenges set before it. Its success clearly stems from its advanced preparations. And the essay concludes with three suggestions for bolstering future planning efforts so to make effective transitions a hallmark of governing from the American nerve center.

TWO OPERATIONAL DILEMMAS, SIX TRANSITION STANDARDS

Despite the extraordinary public attention paid them, presidential transitions have no roadmap. This section identifies in detail six milestones for a successful transition. These standards revolve around discipline and effectiveness, the two operational dilemmas facing a chief of staff.

Sources of Standards

During the presidential election of 2000, two parallel efforts tried to identify what constituted a good presidential transition. As indicated earlier, the Bush for President campaign developed a set of guidelines. And a number of scholarly groups, including the Baker Institute, concentrated on devising transition objectives. The evaluation to follow draws on both these efforts, as the two efforts themselves collaborated with each other.[5]

The Bush Transition Plan

Long before the election had become hopelessly muddled, both campaigns began transition planning. For the most part, the Al Gore for President campaign focused its efforts on identifying policy options available to the new administration. Presumably, their planners had already settled on maintaining the basic Clinton White House operation.[6] The George W. Bush for President transition planners, on the other hand, spent considerable time developing information about operations. Their efforts culminated in eight goals adopted in June of 2000:

1. Clearly communicate that we are aggressively preparing to govern, that we are operating without hubris or triumphant partisanship, that we are experienced and not neophytes, that we are ethical, and that we understand that president-elect is not the president until noon on January 20.

2. Select the senior White House staff and an organizational structure and decision-making process by mid-December.

3. Select the cabinet secretaries by Christmas and have them briefed and ready for confirmation hearings by January 8. Also, have in place by Inauguration Day an organization capable of identifying, clearing, and nominating 165 or more people by April 30, which is as many as any recent administration has sent to the Senate by the 100th day.

4. Summarize all cabinet department priorities, issues, and facts, and the campaign promises related to each, in order to prepare the new secretaries for assuming responsibility for their departments.

5. Prepare to proactively reach out to Congress, supporters, trade associations, well-wishers, and job seekers in order to show our interest in them and to connect with them in a manner and according to a timetable that was of our choosing.

6. Develop a preliminary 20-day, 100-day, and 180-day schedule for the president to guide the initial focus for his energies and time.

7. Prepare to present the new administration's proposed budget changes by mid-February.

8. Review the executive order and regulatory issues requiring immediate attention by the new administration.[7]

While many of these goals addressed the whole administration (such as reviewing executive orders and creating a new budget), most of these goals focused directly on White House transition responsibilities.[8]

Scholarly Research

Paralleling these efforts and preceding them by almost a year, several scholarly organizations developed information on effective transitions and White House operations.[9] For example, based on its extensive interviews with previous staffers, including former chiefs of staff, the White House 2001 Project developed a planning document, *Meeting the Freight Train Head On,* which identified five goals for a successful presidential transition.[10] These included: concentrating on the personnel process, avoiding counterproductive commitments, focusing on selecting the White House staff first, learning from predecessors, and developing a strategic agenda.

The White House 2001 Project developed briefing materials emphasizing a number of transition themes. Their briefing materials underscored Dick Cheney's assessment: "[T]he process of moving paper in and out of the Oval

Office, who gets involved in the meetings, who does the president listen to, who gets a chance to talk to him before he makes a decision is absolutely critical. It has to be managed in such a way that it has integrity."[11] These materials emphasized the importance of "orchestrating" decision opportunities in order to maximize the president's time.[12]

Table 1 combines and summarizes these transition goals and organizes them in relation to the operational dilemmas chiefs of staff must face.

TABLE 1. TRANSITION CHALLENGES, GOALS, AND STANDARDS

DISCIPLINE: The transition should build and then reflect a balance between initiative and orchestration, creativity and control. The goals include:

    1. *Personnel.* Create an effective personnel system.
        a. Overcome the challenge of scale and scrutiny.
        b. Finalize the critical White House staff by mid-December (day 38), including: chief of staff, director OMB, national security advisor, personnel director, legislative affairs director, White House counsel, press secretary.
        c. Finalize the cabinet by Christmas (day 47).
        d. Fill out the administration by nominating 165 policy positions in the government by April 30, 2001.
    2. *Balance.* Develop a balanced White House staff.
        a. Balance out the requirements of Washington experience and knowing the president-elect.
        b. Maintain the "professional" staff by avoiding campaign commitments to reduce White House staff.
    3. *Process.* Develop a White House decision-making system that affords the staff input yet facilitates timely presidential decisions.
        a. By early December, begin using a staff process similar to one suitable for White House use.
        b. Ensure participation by staff and cabinet in decision making.
        c. Develop and enforce a process for orchestrating decisions.

EFFECTIVENESS: The transition should establish a capacity for handling the president's routine decision making and projecting the president's ability into the future.

    4. *Focus.* Maintain focus on the president's agenda.
        a. Develop a 100- and 180-day plan.
        b. Use the plan to structure the president's schedule.
        c. Use the plan to deflect supporters from alternative agendas.
    5. *Crisis.* Maintain a capacity for crisis management.
    6. *Planning.* Think into the future.
        a. Develop a senior planning group.
        b. Maintain that planning function.
        c. Plan for presidential rhythms and for governing.

In effect, this operational dilemma pits personnel against process. The operational challenge: how to tap the energy of White House staff without allowing that energy to interfere with the president's decision making? A disciplined staff depends upon establishing in the transition two important elements—the process through which the president secures a staff and the basic operations necessary to further the president's agenda. This operational dilemma thus produced three identifiable transition goals: selection, balance, and process.

Selection

In talking with the White House Interview Program about successful transitions, former chief of staff (and Forum participant) Dick Cheney underscored the significance of personnel: "You don't have an administration until you staff up—until you go out and you hire people to fill those key slots, recruit a cabinet, [and] fill all those cabinet posts. There are obviously several thousand appointed positions that the president has to fill and if he doesn't fill them or if he accepts whoever was there when he arrived in those positions or if he selects bad people, his administration is not going to be successful."[13] Establishing a selection process presents a number of challenges for a president-elect's team. This section underscores four: scale, staffing, cabinet, and government.

Scale. Above all else, the transition personnel system must have the capacity to simultaneously process the large number of incoming applications while locating and recruiting short lists of candidates. The challenge seems apparent: as part of the governor's office, for example, the Texas appointments unit maintained a database of potential nominees similar to what they would need in the transition. As the country's second-largest state, the Texas operation represents something as close to the "big leagues" as governing gets among the states. That database carried about fifteen thousand names. According to those who have gone through it before, in the twenty-four-hour period following election day, the transition can expect as many as ten thousand applications.[14] In just one day, the new operation would receive two-thirds of the total Texas volume. By the end of the truncated presidential transition, the George W. Bush White House system actually carried some sixty thousand applications—four times their previous experience!

One former White House assistant experienced in personnel work said that scale further complicates the process by simply multiplying problems: "People are so paranoid and so atavistic during this period. It's as if there's one lifeboat left and everyone's trying to get on it. . . . People just go crazy."[15] And craziness tends to reinforce itself. Former Bush White House personnel director Chase

Untermeyer describe the problem by noting that once potential nominees lose touch with the White House, they begin calling to check on progress. Then returning those calls becomes part of the growing burden on the personnel staff. Missed phone calls generate more phone inquiries and the list of confused applicants grows exponentially over time.[16] Scale turns on itself and magnifies the difficulties.

Staffing. Picking the White House staff early has a special impact on the administration's transition. Fulfilling that goal makes it easier to accomplish other goals, such as setting national economic policy or selecting the cabinet. For that reason, and upon reflection, President Clinton's first chief of staff, Mr. McLarty, told his fellow chiefs of staff that the early decision to postpone staffing the Clinton White House until they had selected most of the cabinet "was a mistake" (see "Starting the White House"). While the Bush transition goals established targeted dates for selecting both White House staff and the cabinet, they set the final date for staff nine days earlier than the target for completing the cabinet. They thus underscored the fact to which Mr. McLarty alluded: a successful transition depends upon settling the White House staff early.

Cabinet. As Dick Cheney points out, staffing the White House represents the beginning of process, while staffing the cabinet represents the beginnings of policy. Every candidate and president-elect lauds the notion of "cabinet government," not as recognition of teamwork; certainly no president ever imagines "collegial leadership" in the administration. Instead, the notion of cabinet government finds its perennial appeal in the recognition of two pragmatic realities. First, the scope of American government stretches well beyond the interests or commitments of any one elected leader. And, second, the White House never takes the time or develops the expertise to delve into the arcane arts of implementation. In the cabinet, the president places ultimate responsibility for scope and implementation. Establishing the outlines of that cabinet early in the transition sets the course on many relevant but not priority issues. For their transition, the Bush campaign set "by Christmas" as the deadline for finalizing their cabinet appointments, leaving the newly selected secretary-designates a comfortable three weeks to prepare themselves for governing.

Policy Government. If the cabinet constitutes the administration's collective "management," providing the aggregate mechanism for coping with complexity in day-to-day policy implementation, then the "policy government" constitutes the legs on which that management stands. The Bush campaign planners identified a set of policy makers in agencies critical to pushing the president's agenda. As an objective, they set the 100-day mark as the critical milestone for nominating this policy government.

Balance

The chiefs of staff at the Forum noted the often-surprising differences between running for office and governing (see "Starting the White House"). Running against an opponent requires a set of habits different from those needed to govern with that same opponent. In their minds, then, resolving the tension between finding positions for key campaign workers and bringing in those who have had distinguished Washington careers becomes a critical transitional balancing act. Those with an appreciation for the candidate and the campaign play a critical role in the White House since the president's assistants hold fundamentally political jobs. They "keep the flame," remembering the commitments that got them elected. They also have a critical perspective on the president's style. Clay Johnson recalls that after the election, he would help new staff interpret the president-elect's intentions based on his long association with the man. For example, in remembering Andrew Card's transition, Mr. Johnson recalled:

> [Card] asked some questions when he first came in that somebody that had worked around him [Bush] a long time wouldn't have had to ask. Andy would say, "The president-elect wants this to be done. . . . That's not a good idea."
>
> We'd say, "Okay, that's what he wants done, but if you have a good idea, go back and say, 'But, au contraire.' He doesn't want you to just rubber-stamp what he says if you have another idea."
>
> "I know that he said that," Andy would reply, "but does he really mean it?"
>
> "Yes," I'd say, "he really does mean that."[17]

While the campaign staff knows the president, others understand the Washington experience. They provide the critical perspectives necessary to restructure campaign attitudes and routines into governing habits. While the Washington hands spend their transition wondering how literally they should take the new president, the president's closest associates spend a good deal of their time wondering how to get things done in Washington. One close Bush associate characterized his most common transition statement as, "That *can't* be the way that it is done! Is it?" Clearly, presidents need both kinds of experiences, a balance between specialties.

The "professional staff" of the White House offers another, distinctive expertise, one often overlooked by a new administration.[18] Secretary Card noted that a new White House has "an expectation that anyone who worked in the White House was there because of politics when the truth is the [professional staff] were not." He pointed out that the Clinton transition "pull[ed] the plug on a lot of those people and it took them some time to get back up to speed and it also invited distrust."[19] Many of the former chiefs of staff agreed with Card's assessment. James A. Baker III recalled during the Forum that Secretaries Rumsfeld and Cheney had both recommended to him that in the Reagan transition he should "keep those people, don't think about moving them around, don't worry about their politics; they're basically apolitical; they know their jobs" (see "Starting the White House").

Process

A White House staff without an orderly decision-making process threatens the president's policy agenda by undermining smooth operations. No one can appreciate that fact more than the White House chief of staff. Indeed, as Congressman Panetta pointed out during the Forum, sometimes only the chief of staff understands the necessity for this operational requirement. James A. Baker III summarized the problem: "You have to make sure you have an orderly system, that you have a system that's fair. Otherwise, you start the leaking in the press one against the other."[20] Many of the former chiefs agreed that how you organize presidential decisions leads ultimately to less internal conflict, fewer internal disputes leaking into the public arena, and more candid and therefore effective advice.

Effectiveness

This element of a transition pits the ability of the White House to handle issues in the present while projecting the president's agenda into the future. It entails three challenges: focus, crisis, and planning.

Focus

The presidential transition offers a wonderful opportunity for an administration to realize its policy agenda. "The early months are so important," observed David Gergen, a senior official in both Democratic and Republican White Houses. "[T]hat's when you have the most authority, but that's when you also have the least capacity for making the right decisions."[21] While they become familiar with the new president, the public and even political opponents willingly grant the administration some running room. "There is a coming together after an election that is a natural and wonderful impulse in America," observed James Cicconi, former White House staff secretary.[22]

Using that running room, however, requires advanced planning that accomplishes two objectives. First, the administration must use the transition time to "schedule backwards": identify presidential objectives and build into their governing activities the time necessary to fully articulate the policy initiatives those objectives imply. Putting a transition plan in place and scheduling backwards clarifies what kind of preparation the new administration's goals require. For example, a week before the Clinton team arrived at the White House, one of the president-elect's key advisors, George Stephanopoulos, asked the Office of Management and Budget to prepare a new presidential budget by altering the budget document waiting for release from the previous administration. He wanted the new presidential budget made public on Monday, five days following President Clinton's inauguration. OMB staff responded that while they did not oppose making the requested changes, they simply could not meet the schedule. "It wasn't that if they stretched real hard," recalls a Clinton White House staffer familiar with the budget negotiations, "they could get it, although that was sort of the first thing everybody in the White House [thought]. . . . [Y]ou can't share [changes] with the agencies, manage the process . . . so it ticks and ties and put it all back into the computers, print the appendices. You couldn't do all of that in a week. I think we settled ultimately on something like the twenty-first of February. It was three weeks and it was a stretch." While campaigns work on instant schedules and rapid responses, policy making must withstand the intense scrutiny and organized and long-term opposition that governing involves. Governing obliges far-flung coordination as well as sophisticated presentation. It involves the persistence of the long-distance runner, not the power of the sprinter.

Second, the new administration must maintain a policy focus on what it has in mind, often in spite of sophisticated pressures to the contrary. A new administration comes to Washington as just the latest entrant into what the permanent community of interests and decision makers sees as a continuous parade. The public has certified the administration's authority, but the Washington community has designs on the uses of that authority. And, they have had more experience pursuing their goals than the new president's team has had in pursuing its. The former chiefs of staff agreed that maintaining an effective pursuit of the administration's policy goals constitutes one of the transition's critical challenges. Often, accomplishing this goal depends as much on avoiding the entreaties of friends as it does sidestepping the traps set by opponents.

For this reason, many of the former chiefs of staff recommended a technique pioneered by the Reagan transition. Under the guidance of Reagan pollster Richard Wirthlin and based on a detailed historical study directed by David Gergen, the transition team developed a plan outlining their initial daily activities.[23] The Gergen study surveyed transitions in six major categories: constitutional, foreign affairs, domestic affairs, domestic appearances, press and media appearances, and miscellaneous.[24] Using this plan afforded the Reagan White House a clear set of activities designed to support their immediate focus on economic recovery and regulatory reform. While these plans resembled a campaign plan, with daily messages and activities projected through the first weeks of the administration, the overall effort clarified their objectives and gave them a convenient reference point from which to "refocus" the agendas of friends and foe alike.

Crisis

The former chiefs of staff had a great deal to say about the challenges of crisis management. That would make sense, since a full one-third of them came to office in the midst of a crisis and many others experienced one. Most of them agreed with Mack McLarty, who emphasized that a White House must "try to segment [a crisis] and separate it as much as you possibly can and isolate it."[25] Additionally, the former chiefs of staff agreed with Howard Baker, Jr., that in a crisis, the White House staff must get the president onto a vigorous schedule in order to restore the administration's momentum for governing (see "Refocusing the White House").

Planning

Speaking to the White House 2001 Project and reflecting on his previous experiences, Secretary Card specifically identified the lack of forward planning on the president's behalf as a critical weakness: "We tried [to plan for the long range]. We tried and tried and tried. We tried to have a sense of historic events or a political calendar or a congressional calendar. We desperately tried to have a vision to what we were doing. We failed, in my opinion."[26] Other former chiefs of staff have also found that the pressures of the present undermine planning. Note, for example, James Baker's reflections on the lack of planning after the initial Reagan transition plan expired: "[Y]ou really are putting out fires and you're a lot more 'reactive' than you are 'proactive' and that's just the nature of the beast."[27]

Of course, establishing an intention to plan and designating staff to plan does not assure planning. Handling the day-to-day action—"reactive" management—usually demands all the attention of the senior staff, which often relegates the planning function to junior assistants. Plans made by assistants often get short shrift from principals when considered in the heat of decision making.[28] To accomplish effective planning, the White House must establish a high-level staff group, composed of senior advisors.

As Secretary Card noted, White House strategic planning has two central elements: historic events and political timetables (including the congressional schedule). Historic events include those special initiatives that the White House understands to define their administration. Such initiatives may surface in the president's State of the Union address and stretch through the spring into the summer. Then the congressional calendar tends to take over Washington. Late in the spring, the Congress begins to focus on the budget, with its first Congressional Budget Resolution leading to consideration of the general authorization legislation. While the president's schedule tends to focus on foreign policy commitments during these authorization/summer months, both schedules reorient themselves as the Congress begins consideration of its appropriation bills. Simultaneously, the executive branch considerations of the next fiscal year's budget requests and the organizing work for the president's State of the Union speech begin to build to a climax near the end of the congressional session. Without serious reflection on what Martha J. Kumar calls these "rhythms of the president's year," a White House abdicates some of its control over the agenda. Then "time" makes presidential decisions. Thinking into the future provides a White House counterweight to the inevitable leverage of congressional routines. White House planning should therefore take into account these presidential rhythms.

Using congressional routine as a foil for planning, however, does not represent the goal of White House plans. Instead, as Secretary Card notes, planning must create a vision of direction. Given the press of reactive management, pushing the White House horizon ahead just one week often constitutes a serious achievement. Yet serious and effective planning requires projecting the administration's horizon to months ahead. The further their horizon projects, though, the more complicated and unpredictable the interactions and the less attractive planning becomes for senior staff inundated with more pressing demands. Elections, of course, represent convenient temporal horizons punctuated at two-year intervals. Given their contradictory requirements, though, planning for elections gainsays planning for governing. The nature of planning becomes an inherently interesting and charged process with no well-established conventional wisdom.

ASSESSING THE BUSH TRANSITION

When it comes to governing, intentions and performance often diverge.

This section evaluates the George W. Bush transition by comparing its performance against the six common transition goals identified earlier and by using the measures that these goals might suggest. This assessment does not evaluate the Bush administration's policy achievements. The president's effectiveness, translating operations into presidential "success" or "impact," remains a subject for retrospective judgments with the aid of considerably more evidence than currently available. The former chiefs of staff agreed, however, that without effective operations, no administration could succeed even assessed against its own objectives.

Goal 1. Create an Effective Personnel Process

Recall this goal presents four separate standards: scale; White House first; then cabinet; and then the core governing group.

Analyzing the transition personnel goals employs two separate sources of data. First, it relies on official announcements of nominations. Note that administrations never make clear to the public when they decide on the selection of key people. Instead, the outside world can only observe the announcement of these appointments. For these announcements, the *Washington Post* and the *New York Times* became the journals of record. For subcabinet policy positions, the analysis relied on the date of nomination as reported by the Brookings Institution's Presidential Appointee Initiative, which tracked and reported appointment data on the Bush administration. Second, the assessment of staff balance, in particular Goal 2a, relies on data collected by Martha J. Kumar and published in her study, "Establishing a White House."[29]

Handling Scale

To handle scale, the Bush planners focused on candidate assessment. In particular, early in the transition planning and well in advance of their convention, they decided on new technologies for handling the staggering flow of applicants. The Clinton transition team had pioneered a "labor intensive" plan by recruiting 40 professional headhunters working as volunteers and backed up by a sizable support staff. These volunteers, 125 in all, recruited and then vetted candidates with a record-keeping system that involved scanning hard-copy resumes. That operation did not translate into the White House, as the relatively sizable transition staff shrank precipitously to the number permitted in the presidency. In addition, by relying on the untried technology of transforming optical images into text, the Clinton team fell hopelessly behind, at one point in the transition simply throwing out three thousand applications sitting in its backlog in a frustrated effort to "catch up."

The Bush team opted for a capital-intensive plan requiring applicants to enter resumes on a website that automatically fed into the transition's database. This approach reduced the need for a large transition staff ("It got us out of the data entry business," Clay Johnson noted) and relied instead on a staff similar in size to what they would have in office. This system easily accumulated applications without having to manage its growth. The system also allowed the staff to judge applicants without consideration of patrons or references. In some instances, the White House filled positions by simply searching for appropriate candidates from those applications that had "come in over the transom." This electronic and capital-intensive approach had produced a database of about seventy thousand entries by the end of the transition and constituted a genuinely effective effort at addressing scale.[30]

White House

Table 2 reports results on finalizing the White House staff by day 38—goal 1b. The table compares the Bush transition personnel announcements to the average announcement dates for the previous four presidential transitions. The table compares two groups of staff: "critical" and "core." Critical staff are those positions identified in the White House 2001 Project's study *Meeting the Freight Train Head On.* Core staff are the critical staff plus the director of the White House Office of Management and Administration, the staff secretary, and the director of communications.

As indicated in the table, the Bush transition missed its initial goal, which in this case would have occurred a mere three days after the conclusion of the contested Florida election. Their performance overshot their objective for the core staff by about seven days (–6.8). On the other hand, they announced their critical staff almost eleven days (–10.8) earlier than the typical presidential transition.

Since the opportunity for completing the staff has a lower bound, at zero days, and an upper bound, say at the 100-day mark, we can assess performance in terms of "efficiency" or how well the 2001 transition improved on the previous record of transitions, adjusted for these upper and lower bounds.[31] Thus, we can conclude from the data that the 2001 transition improved on the previous experiences by +16 percent for the critical staff and +10 percent for the core staff. Using the normal standard for what constitutes a "significant" improvement (± 10 percent), the 2001 transition made significant improvements over the average despite their hampered beginnings with the Florida recount. Indeed, their experience constitutes the second quickest transition for both core and critical staffs (the first Bush administration set the record at day 44 for both categories). The average administration finalized its staff around day 69, with Republicans slightly earlier on average than Democrats. Governor Bush's decision to invest in transition planning clearly paid dividends in White House staff readiness.

TABLE 2. ANNOUNCEMENT OF WHITE HOUSE STAFF (IN DAYS AFTER ELECTION)

Type of White House Position	Administration(s) and Averages			Difference between Bush and Previous		
	Previous administrations			Bush	Bush	Improvement
	Both Parties	GOP	DEM			
Critical staff	68.8	65.0	72.5	58.0	−10.8	16%
Chief of staff	19.3			10.0	−9.3	
National security advisor	39.8			40.0	0.2	
Director OMB	29.8			45.0	15.2	
Legislative affairs	57.8			58.0[a]	0.2	
Personnel	40.5			52.0	11.5	
Counsel	58.0			40.0	−18.0	
Press secretary	42.0			51.0	9.0	
Core staff	68.8	65.0	72.5	62.0	−6.8	10%

Source: Compiled by Terry Sullivan from Lexis/Nexis, *Washington Post,* and *New York Times.*

[a]On Nov. 29, 2000, the transition announced that David Gribben would head congressional relations. Around Christmas, however, Mr. Gribben became sidelined with a painful eye problem. On Jan. 4, 2001, the Bush team announced his replacement, Nicholas Calio (see Judy Sarosohn, "Calio Likely to Join Bush Team as Lobbyist," Washington Post, Jan. 4, 2001, p. A19). This position was therefore considered open until Jan. 4, 2001.

Cabinet

Table 3 summarizes the transition's experience with its cabinet goal—goal 1c: announcing the cabinet by December 24, 2000 ("by Christmas Day," or day 47). Again the figures detail the differences between the Bush transition personnel announcements and the average for the previous presidential transitions. These data cover appointments of two separate groups: the "core" cabinet and the "full" cabinet.

As the table suggests, the Bush transition did a remarkable job of making cabinet appointments in a timely manner. Even though they missed their Christmas goal, they fell short of that goal for the full cabinet by a mere nine days despite the truncated transition. And, while their core cabinet announcements trailed the average, they completed the entire cabinet two days earlier than the average presidential transition. The loss and gains of efficiency for selecting the core and full cabinet, respectively, appear modest for the Bush transition at around ± 3 percent. The Bush final cabinet announcement (at day 56) lay between the typical Democratic completion date of day 51 and the standard Republican completion date of day 64. Thus, despite the hurdles presented by the unusual circumstances, the Bush transition did better than any previous Republican transition and only slightly worse than those transitions that admittedly focused exclusively on cabinet recruitment.

Policy Leadership

The details of this goal appear somewhat elusive. In setting it, the Bush transition planners clearly wanted to underscore the importance of quickly filling out the government's policy-making apparatus. The standard they set for themselves seems to refer to merely getting as many nominations out the door as any previous administration had. However, the target they selected (165 appointments) does come very close to a specific definition of the policy leadership. The examination here will first evaluate the simple motivation of filling a record number of positions and then evaluate their performance against two definitions of the policy leadership.

Considering the first interpretation of their goal—large numbers—their record seems reasonable. By April 30, 2001, the Bush White House had nomi-

TABLE 3. ANNOUNCEMENT OF CABINET
(IN DAYS AFTER ELECTION)

Type of Cabinet Position	Administration(s) and Averages				Difference between Bush and Previous	
	Previous administrations			Bush	Bush	Improvement
	Both parties	GOP	DEM			
Core	45.3	41.0	50.0	51.0	5.7	−4%
Defense	43.5			51.0	7.5	
State	31.0			39.0	8.0	
Treasury	30.8			43.0	12.3	
Justice	37.3			45.0	7.7	
Commerce	38.0			43.0	5.0	
Full	57.5	64.0	51.0	56.0	−1.5	3%

Source: Compiled by Terry Sullivan from *Washington Post, New York Times,* and others.

nated 180 positions. Around 40 of those nominations, however, came from "holdovers" asked to remain at their posts.[32] Without these holdover appointments, the administration would not have reached its simple goal of 165 appointments.

Consider a different definition of their goal, though, one focusing on the "coverage" of these 165 nominations. For the purposes of that assessment, the following two standards will define a critical policy-making position as listed in the 1996 *Plum Book:*

> a. *Appointment Type:* Policy-making positions require Senate confirmation, i.e., they have a "PAS" classification
> b. *Pay Plan and Grade:* Policy-making positions carry an Executive classification, i.e., listed as "EX," and a pay grade of at least Level III.[33]

The two standards encompass the leadership of all cabinet departments, all independent regulatory agencies (such as the Federal Reserve), and all independent agencies delivering services (such as the Agency for International Development). Using these two criteria, PAS EW-I/III, generates a list of about 170 positions, very close to the 165 in the transition goal. By eliminating from that list appointments with statutory tenures that did not expire until after the April 30 deadline, the number drops to 137 positions. So, in effect, if the goal is to Wll out the policy-making apparatus of the government, that would require filling 137 specific positions before April 30, 2001.[34]

Table 4 summarizes the Bush White House experience Wlling out the policy leadership. The administration filled 68 of those positions by its deadline, or about one-half of the goal of 137. The table also presents an alternative target that reflects some later thinking in the White House. In interviews with Professor Martha J. Kumar, White House staff familiar with the transition indi-

TABLE 4. EXECUTIVE APPOINTMENTS FILLED BY DAY 100

Objective	Positions		
	Potential	Filled	
EX I/III	170	—	—
Without term mandates	137	68	50%
"Big Four" cabinet	58	47	81%

Source: Compiled by Terry Sullivan from Presidential Appointee Initiative statistics.

cated that after Florida, they adjusted their goal, settling on a different strategy for handling appointments than the broader ambition identified in June. This new strategy emphasized the selection of "central positions" in each cabinet agency. Once confirmed, the department principals would fill out the remaining positions. Using this so-called "Big Four" strategy (referring to the secretary, deputy secretary, assistant secretary, and press secretary), the Bush White House supposed that it could balance its need for control with its cabinet's interest in delegation.[35] Taking that goal instead of the one adopted earlier for the transition, the number of positions to fill drops to 58.[36] Clearly, the Bush administration did a better job with this more limited goal. It filled 81 percent of those Big Four positions by the one hundredth day. Unfortunately, no similar statistics exist for previous administrations with which to compare this performance.

Summary

Without considering the truncated transition, the Bush White House made remarkable progress towards meeting the personnel requirements of the transition. It set records in filling out its White House staff and cabinet. And under some (but not all) measures it made seemingly significant progress in filling the central policy-making positions in government.

Goal 2. A Balanced Staff

This general transition goal set two standards: a balanced staff (between campaign and Washington) and protecting the "professional" White House staff.

Balance of Expertise

While no comparisons exist with other administrations, some data allow for examining the Bush balance in absolute terms. Table 5 outlines the experience of thirty-three key White House staff identified by Martha J. Kumar.[37] It divides relevant experience into five categories ranging from purely personal to purely Washington. The first two categories in the table, "personal" (knowledge of the president, his work habits, etc.) and "campaign" (work in the presidential campaign) constitute important attributes of about 60 percent of these critical White House staff. By contrast, knowledge of the White House or of policy substance constitutes an attribute of only around 40 percent of the staff. Thus, the staff seems weighted towards campaign and personal associations with the president, seeming to reinforce James A. Baker's observation at the Forum that "when you are replacing an administration of the other party, you look to the campaign more often to get the people that are going to come into the White House" (see "Starting the White House").

Looking at the overlap between knowledge bases affords a sense of staff balance. For example, of those with campaign experience, only one-quarter also have some policy-specific experience, while three-quarters had some prior personal association with Governor Bush. By comparison, those with campaign experience who had prior White House staff experience amounts to a very small number, seven, a bit more than 20 percent. Those with prior White House experience but having no campaign or personal association with the president-elect constitute those staff recruited by the chief of staff to round out the new team's experience base. These specialized and balancing appointments focused on critical operational elements, including congressional relations and White House administration. In general, "Washington hands" (those with either prior White House or Washington experience) played a critical role in the transition. White House staff with only personal experience reported they found their instincts did not jibe with the routines of the Capitol and without the special advice of the Washington staff they would have taken serious missteps.

One additional element of this balance seems worth noting. Only four of the thirty-three staff had extensive experience in all of the critical categories discussed here (campaign, personal, White House, Washington): Card, Josh Bolton, Joseph Hagin, and Lawrence Lindsey. These four, three in the chief of staff's office, constitute the overlapping core between all of the various forms of knowledge necessary for a smooth White House transition. They constitute the hub in the governing wheel.

TABLE 5. EXPERTISE OF TOP WHITE HOUSE STAFF

| | Base of Knowledge | | | | |
	Campaign	Personal	Policy	White House	Purely D.C.
Number	20	19	11	12	15
Percent	61%	58%	33%	36%	45%
Overlaps (number)	15	4		8	

Source: Adapted from Kumar, "Establishing a White House Staff," chart 1.

Professional Staff

As part of their strategies for defending themselves from charges of promising "big-spending government," Democratic candidates have promised to shrink their White House staffs. Typical among these Democratic candidates, both Jimmy Carter and Bill Clinton promised to reduce the White House staff by 25 percent. Once in office, of course, the reality of maintaining the president's advisors means that in order to make good on this promise the new president must reduce the professional staff supporting operations. Reductions among these staff have generally undermined the White House's ability to function. "Frankly," noted Roy Neel, "the only [people] who cared about that [promise] in 1992 were a handful that populate the House Government Operations Committee *on the other side*. It never made any sense to do that. They're designed to get you some press but . . . they come back to haunt you" (emphasis added).[38]

Unlike Al Gore, candidate Bush did not promise to reduce the White House staff during the campaign. As a result, Secretary Card saw little need to change the staffing patterns already in place among the professional staff.

Summary

On this transition measure, the George W. Bush White House performed well. The transition produced a staff with a good mix between the needed White House specialties. Some of that balance derived directly from recruitment of people outside of the governor's campaign group. In addition, the Bush campaign and then transition maintained a solid foundation of professional support in the White House.

Goal 3. A Disciplined Process

This goal rested on two objectives: early experience with disciplined decision making and balanced access and orchestration.

Experience

Maintaining discipline requires experience with White House proportions. The Bush for President senior staff determined to build a working White House operation before they had to bear the responsibilities of governing. Adopting such a system early, Clay Johnson thought, would give them the experience many of them would need. He thought practice would act as a good antidote to the scrutiny they would all receive once in office. Card independently determined to begin a senior staff schedule to mirror the early morning White House schedule. According to Johnson, the "White House" senior staff began meeting December 12 in a regular, daily ritual involving an early morning, thirty-minute senior staff meeting much like those they would regularly attend in the White House.[39] The transition met this goal.

Access and Timing

The former chiefs of staff participating in the Forum appreciated that the contrasting pressures for individual accomplishment and orderly decisions constitute the two poles in a well-run White House. Evaluating the degree to which such a balance exists can prove difficult since any White House naturally prefers to avoid such scrutiny. However, the imbalances created when these two sides of discipline collide rather than coexist generate signs visible from afar. When White House staff begin to feel excluded from decision making or the balance between their interests and those of an effective process shifts, they begin venting their frustrations extramurally. They participate in news stories acting as "insiders" or as "unnamed sources," often airing disagreements to the outside world but, more importantly, simply conveying their alternative focuses. Thus, the number of stories relying on anonymous "White House sources" constitutes one crude measure of imbalance or lack of focus.

TABLE 6. INSIDER SOURCES IN NEWS STORIES

Administration	Days	Unnamed Source in White House		Unnamed Source in Administration	
Carter	100	7		12	
	180	8		20	
	365	15		38	
Reagan	100	18		28	
	180	25		41	
	365	36		80	
Bush, GHW	100	2		27	
	180	5		36	
	365	7		66	
Clinton	100	4		13	
	180	8		21	
	365	14		33	
			avg. of previous administrations		avg. of previous administration
Bush, GW	100	0	7.8	5	20.0
	180	0	11.5	10	29.5
	365	0	18.0	11	54.3

Source: Compiled by Terry Sullivan from Lexis/Nexis searches.

Table 6 summarizes stories printed in the two major newspapers most often used for Washington communications (the *New York Times* and the *Washington Post*). Data collection occurred during three standard periods of an administration: the first 100 days, the first 180 days, and the first year. The table divides unnamed sources into two categories: those inside the "White House" and those inside the "administration." As the table makes very clear, the George W. Bush White House maintained an historic level of focus during their entire first year. While a new administration might have as many as eighteen stories on average during its first year, members of the Bush White House did not participate in a single story. "The people who control the channels of communication have their egos carefully under control," notes former speechwriter David Frum. "They have fewer psychodramas than any staff since the invention of staff." In discussing this aspect of their administration (the lack of "psychodrama"), Karl Rove described the situation in terms that clearly reflect their attention to focus. He noted that among Bush's senior advisors, when advocating "a perspective diametrically opposed to the point of view of the person on the sofa across from [you]," the senior staff knows that they will "link arms and go on, and be certain that your losing view won't appear in the paper."[40]

Three elements seem to stand out in avoiding the internal disputes of previous administrations. As expected, each of these keys to process reinforce the importance of orderly (even orchestrated) decision making. First, Chief of Staff Card divided White House management between two deputy chiefs of staff, one managing policy and one managing "mechanics." Pioneered by Thomas McLarty in the second year of the Clinton administration as an attempt to rein in Clinton's chaotic and often esoteric decision-making process, the division of responsibilities between two deputies allows for more rigorous attention to the orchestration of decisions by concentrating the distracting responsibilities for mechanics into a separate office. Freed to coordinate with the staff secretary, the chief of staff and his chief deputy for policy can spend more time on assuring the process. While the use of this division did not take hold in the Clinton administration until the chief of staff changed, Card's emphasis on this approach has undergirded the integrity of that process.

Second, Card highlighted the work of their staff secretary, whose diligence has reassured presidential advisors and cabinet that the process will not exclude their views from proper consideration. Harriet Miers focuses incessantly on assuring balance, Card says: "'That's one view, where's the other?' Or 'this looks like it was written by Larry Lindsey; I want to make sure Glen Hubbard has a chance to see it.'"[41]

Third, Card underscores his emphasis on both initiation and orchestration. He regularly makes clear that staff and critical administration officials can expect to get their views before the president. Since the principal temptation to shirk discipline stems from a growing sense of exclusion, Card emphasizes that cabinet and advisors have guaranteed access to the president whenever they *need* that attention to their advice. At the same time, he makes clear that *needing* and *wanting* to see the president are not the same thing. After all, Card notes, "there are an infinite number of great ideas in Washington, and nearly an infinite number of people willing to give those ideas to the president, so what you have to do is decide what the president needs to have and then find a way to fit it into a day in such a way that he has an ability to make a sound decision."[42]

This system has antecedents in other administrations. Card's approach resembles the system in place when he began his White House service during the Reagan administration. That system guaranteed access to cabinet officers through a post office box for the president's exclusive use, along with an accompanying guarantee that any cabinet officer could get access to the president with twenty-four-hours notice. The George H. W. Bush White House, where Card also worked, maintained a similar box for guaranteed cabinet access. Former Clinton chief of staff John Podesta emphasized how such a system made "key decision makers both in the cabinet and in the White House feel like they have access to the president and that they're part of the team and that if they have a strong view, it's being represented and is not getting shut out by some filter." Podesta went on to note that if the system fails these key actors, then the White House would "end up with just a lot of cranky people who are going to act out in destructive ways. White Houses have died on that basis."[43]

While similar in approach to others, the decision system Card created works partly because so many of the critical White House staff positions have fallen to individuals long associated with the president and with little independent Washington experience: "They've had a longer relationship with George Bush than others have had with a president," Card notes.[44] That balance has made for a keener identification with the president's interests by comparison with independent or external agendas and a stronger sense of confidence in the president's trust. To some extent, then, this transition result may rest on the unusual expertise of the Bush White House. Given that the president can find only a limited number of potential staff with similar close associations, the chief of staff will likely face a problem reinventing this extraordinary discipline as the initial staff retires and a newer staff arrives without these unique associations.

Summary

The Bush staff established a decision process that served them well throughout the transition. Practiced and honed after the election decision, White House routines allowed advisors and cabinet a sense of access without sacrificing the discipline of orchestrated policy making.

Goal 4. Focused Agenda

This goal suggested three measures: the development of a detailed transition plan, using that plan to schedule the administration's initial activities and policy, and using the plan to deflect alternative agenda strategies, including those of political allies.

Developing a Plan

While Andy Card focused on planning White House operations, chief political strategist Karl Rove began developing a governing plan. Like Card's activities, Rove's research proceeded parallel to the Florida legal efforts. Unlike Card's activities that depended heavily on his White House experiences, Rove's planning began with a search for information about what to expect using previous transitions. Using the Gergen system, Rove assigned six staff members each to research the first one hundred days of a previous transition.[45] Their research phase concluded December 8, 2000, four days before the final Supreme Court decision. Their preliminary plan went to the president-elect on December 15, 2000, only three days after the senior staff began meeting with their "practice" White House routine. By the first week of January, 2001, the transition team had drafted a detailed plan for the first weeks, a less-detailed plan through March, and a general plan through the August congressional recess. This increasing generality allowed White House planners to elaborate plans as they became more familiar with governing.

Rove's research team created a "matrix" of indicators, from which they developed a sense of "what were [the previous transitions] attempting to do?" Their study developed data on a range of activities from the average number of press conferences to the number of policy initiatives.[46] "We looked at that matrix," remembers Rove, "and where there were differences [between transitions] we tried to figure out what they were trying to do." The matrix also gave them a sense of what to expect, the "normal and ordinary traffic" cutting into the president's time, and what kind of time they needed to prepare what they planned on doing. In a sense, they tried to construct a picture of presidential activities.[47]

Table 7 presents data consistent with the matrix employed by Rove's planners. It summarizes those topics Rove researched, utilizing data from three sources. The first data derive from statistics reported by Mr. Rove ("R"). Other data summarizes the original Gergen study completed for the 1981 Reagan tran-

TABLE 7. COMPARATIVE STATISTICS ON PRESIDENTIAL TRANSITIONS

	Major Policies	Executive Orders	Messages to Congress	Joint Session Speech	Meetings with			Press Conferences	Television or Other Media	Presidential Travel		
					Congress	Cabinet	Interests			Foreign	Domestic	Time Off
Study Transition	R[a]	S[b]	R/S	S	S/G[c]	S/G	S/G	S/G	S/G	S/G	S/G	S/G
Roosevelt					-/10	-/30	-/2	-/20	-/3	-/0	-/0	-/0
Eisenhower		20	11/11		-/9	-/14	-/3	-/7	-/10	-/0	-/0	-/2
Kennedy	8	23	19/19	2	3/3	2/2	4/4	10/10	7/7	0/0	1/2	0/2
Nixon	7	15	19/19	1	10/15	15/15	5/4	5/6	1/0	1/0	2/3	13/7
Carter	9	16	18/18	2	26/7	15/15	37/12	6/6	3/4	0/0	3/4	7/4
Reagan	8	18	5/8	3	37/-	17/-	35/-	2/-	1/-	0/-	2/-	8/-
GHW Bush	10	11	13/7	2	16/-	4/-	27/-	11/-	0/-	1/-	11/-	9/-
Clinton	4	13	10/7	3	26/-	4/-	27/-	13/-	15/-	1/-	10/-	3/-
Average	7.7	16.6	14.1/12.7	2.2	26.3/-	10.0/-	31.5/-	7.8/-	4.5/-	0.5/-	4.8/-	6.7/-
Error	2.1	4.1	4.3/5.7	0.8	8.6/-	7.0/-	5.3/-	4.2/-	5.7/-	0.5/-	4.4/-	4.6/-
G. W. Bush	4	12	6	2	11	4	28	5	16	2[d]	22[d]	4

[a] R = Rove statistics

[b] S = data compiled by Terry Sullivan from *Congressional Record*, *Public Papers of the President*, and *Weekly Compilation of Presidential Documents*. All data on George W. Bush taken from *Weekly Compilation*.

[c] G = data compiled by Terry Sullivan from Gergen's tables.

[d] Indicates statistically significant difference.

sition ("G").The remaining matrix elements ("S") derive from data collected by the author from what appeared as similar sources. Wherever Rove's partial summaries made comparisons possible (such as "Messages to Congress," "Executive Orders"), these second data appeared consistent with his results. The table also reports data for the 2001 Bush transition.

Starting Policy

On matters of policy, the matrix has some interesting patterns to reveal. "When you look at [policy]," Rove argues, two clear groups of presidents stand out in the matrix: "some presidents come into office with an agenda that they want to pursue in a pretty aggressive fashion. Other presidents come in as 'transitional presidencies,'" those preserving the on-going agenda. In addition, the planners learned from their own analysis that the transition needed to connect its campaign rhetoric directly to the use of the president's discretion, focusing presidential initiatives on central campaign elements. "We looked at what was it that they established in the campaign," Rove notes, "and how did that carry through to the opening scene, if you will?" This section assesses the degree to which the transition plan outlined a policy linked to the campaign agenda.

The use of this planning information resulted in not only the creation of a strategic plan, the subject of the first measure of goal 4, but it orchestrated an unprecedented outpouring of initiatives in the earliest stages of the transition. Though the Bush transition did not adopt a wide array of initiatives, exactly half the average for the three previous Republican transitions, the Bush White House produced *all* of its four major policy messages to Congress by the first week of February, or ending at day 19. By comparison, President Clinton did not produce his first major message (economic) until day 29, a full ten days after the entire Bush agenda had gone to Congress. Two other major proposals by President Clinton—on economic stimulus and national service—did not appear until around day 89. President George H. W. Bush, who campaigned as "the education president," did not produce a message to Congress on education until day 86. And Ronald Reagan, the recognized champion of a focused transition, did not report on his economic package until day 29, again a full ten days after the entire Bush agenda had gone out to the Congress. Clearly, Rove's planning had established a connection between the campaign themes and the action agenda of the administration. That plan had prepared them to satisfy the second measure of transition success in this area, using their plans to promote policy.

Maintaining a Focus

The Bush administration's plan faced three typical challenges that tested their commitment to their own agenda. The first involved the campaign finance proposals of Senator John McCain (R-Ariz.) whose insurgency in the Republican primaries for a while had threatened Governor Bush's presidential hopes. A second incident involved a managed-care proposal from a broad-based coalition of House and Senate members.[48] Both of these proposals diverted attention from the administration's top priority proposals for a tax cut and education reform. Karl Rove worked hard behind the scenes, according to reports, to postpone the health care and election reform agendas in order to maintain attention on the administration's top priorities. On both, the administration managed to maintain their single-minded focus on their plans with assistance from a cooperative Republican congressional party leadership.

On a third issue, the administration faced allies in the private sector determined to take advantage of the president's tax cut initiative. According to reports in March of 2001, dozens of trade organizations and corporations with their own lobbies had instigated a plan to secure favorable tax treatments under the umbrella of tax reform sponsored by the administration. Along with all of the senior members of the president's team, including efforts by Vice President Cheney and White House Chief of Staff Andrew Card, Karl Rove worked "aggressively" to convince these organizations to abandon their own plans and "get with the [Bush] program."[49]

Despite these successes, the administration became its own worst opponent after the House had passed the president's highest priority tax cut at day 48. Almost immediately after this initial legislative success, the White House took a series of actions on the environment, beginning on day 52, that disrupted public focus on the president's agenda. These actions included reversing a campaign promise on carbon dioxide emissions, junking the Kyoto Accords on Global Warming, and initiating a fiasco over the mandatory review of arsenic standards in drinking water. On each of these issues, a considerable amount of notoriety ensued that diverted attention from the administration's tax cut efforts in the Senate.

Summary

Using the data that Rove's transition research uncovered, the Bush transition team gleaned a number of informative lessons. Those lessons, in turn, informed their plans, which proved dramatically useful. That research drove the preparation of the president's early schedule and the presentation of his policy agenda in record time. It further established a foundation for focusing their attention away from those "friendly" distractions presented by the Washington policy community and towards more time expended on the president's agenda. If, as Secretary Baker argued at the beginning of the Forum, the White House has no other objective to governing than policy, the Bush transition made excellent progress towards that objective.

Goal 5. A Capacity for Crisis

This goal established one clear objective: maintaining a flexible decision process.

The transition, itself, did not present a crisis of the size contemplated under this goal. While most administrations face an early test over one of their cabinet appointments, the Bush White House had little in the way of that kind of distraction. Subsequent events in the late transitional period, however, made it clear how the Bush White House approaches crises. In early April, 2001, for example, the president faced a confrontation with China over a midair collision in international air space involving an American intelligence aircraft and a Chinese fighter jet. A few months later, in early September, 2001, an assault on American soil by international terrorists also challenged the administration's decision-making process. In both the Chinese crisis and the 9/11 attack, the Bush White House appears to have adopted one common approach—creating a crisis management team, thereby relieving everyone else of crisis responsibilities. "Walling off" the crisis in this fashion, the former chiefs of staff agreed, represents the best approach to maintaining White House governing functions.

In the Chinese crisis, the administration set up a policy-making group including, from the White House, the national security advisor, the chief of staff, and senior counselor for communications. For the 9/11 attack, the creation of a Homeland Security Office inside the White House walled off the crisis, leaving that office in charge of managing the issue and freeing the rest of the staff to concentrate on their normal responsibilities. As a clear indicator that the White House has employed this strategy, senior Bush aide Karl Rove played no role in the Chinese crisis and Karen Hughes (while on the staff) and Mr. Rove did not participate in the "war crisis" group. Instead, the presence of the crisis team left them to concentrate on their own responsibilities for message and long-term, political planning.[50]

Summary
Although most administrations face an early distraction during the appointments process, the Bush transition received no significant challenges in this regard. Subsequent international crises have demonstrated the administration's capacity to maintain its White House operations through the recommended

strategy of walling off the crisis with a special management group. The 2001 transition presented a textbook case of crisis management, one rarely matched by other transitions.

Goal 6. Think into the Future

This goal hoped to achieve three objectives: identifying a senior planning group, maintaining a planning function, and focusing on the rhythms of governing.

Senior Planning Group

Given the Bush team's proclivities to begin early and to reflect on previous experiences, it seems reasonable to expect that the new White House would place a degree of emphasis on what Card called "forward planning." The Bush White House has utilized a number of planning groups designed to fill this previous deficiency, three of which occupy central roles. First, Card organized a midlevel management group, known as the "Conspiracy of the Deputies," a long-range planning group of deputies from all the White House operational offices. Second, the Bush White House reactivated the Nixon-Reagan-era Office of Strategic Initiatives, run by Barry Jackson, a staff group designed to facilitate the strategic planning functions of a third group dubbed the "Strategery Group" (proving that even Republicans watch *Saturday Night Live*).[51]

This emphasis on planning has two effects. First, it fills an obvious gap Secretary Card underscored as present in every modern White House. "By involving what is a larger-than-normal group of people," Mr. Rove hopes, "we'll be pulling the best talents in the White House into planning. The object is to have a strategic framework . . . brought down to each office by the participants. Everybody in the White House has a role in long-term planning."[52] In effect, every operational group has a serious responsibility in planning White House long-term strategy as well as facing everyday operational problems. As a result, the planning staff does not spend time looking for operational responsibilities that would substitute for planning.

Second, involvement by the broad range of offices in the planning process reinforces the critical impression that everyone on the senior staff plays a role in the president's decision making. For example, in addition to Rove, the Strategery group originally included domestic policy adviser Margaret LaMontagne, then economic adviser Lawrence B. Lindsey, national security adviser Condoleezza Rice, Card and his deputy, Joshua Bolten, then–communications director Karen P. Hughes, communications specialists Margaret Tutwiler and Mary Matalin, then–staff secretary Harriet Miers, and the administration's then–top legislative lobbyist Nicholas Calio. Under Rove's supervision, the Strategery group met weekly in the Eisenhower Building to discuss and brainstorm new initiatives and plans for the president's budget in fiscal year 2003 and the off-year election campaign in 2002 and the eventual reelection campaign in 2004. The creation of these three groups satisfies this first planning requirement.

Maintain the Planning Function

Given the attention focused on daily operations, every White House has a difficult time maintaining a planning function, other than the standard unit maintaining the president's schedule. The Bush White House has maintained a dedicated planning function during its time in office. The development of the "Karen and Karl" group and its successor illustrates further their evolving planning operations under the chief of staff. This weekly planning session with senior advisors and the president developed from "new time" carved out of the president's schedule by the staff's "maturing experience." Given the additional time squeezed from the president's schedule, Card thought it important to invest a good portion of that surplus in further advanced planning. In this way, the White House continues to develop its planning activities, elaborating them and dedicating a continuing and growing portion of the president's time to the subject.

Apply Rhythms to Governing

Finally, the president's schedule must consider the Washington community. Both Card and Rove indicated their constant attention in planning to the normal routines of the congressional schedule, especially to the federal budget cycle. They considered the signposts in the president's schedule as opportunities for communicating with the public, to establish their public agenda by their advanced preparations.

Mr. Rove notes that one implication of this planning for the congressional rhythms allowed them to react to the normal schedule and bend it to their advantage. They believe attention to these rhythms afforded them advantages on those issues most central to their policy agenda. In particular, they believe that attention to these rhythms helped them move their initial tax cut, the center of their policy agenda, through the congressional agenda faster than normal.

Table 8 summarizes data on this claim about planning by reporting the completion of administration initiatives during the first year in office for the 2001 transition and for the previous six transitions. It compares the Bush experience on its tax initiative as well as other major initiatives, those set out in presidential messages to Congress. The data supports Mr. Rove's conclusion that detailed planning moved their tax cut through Congress with alacrity. Of course, some administration critics point out that politicians generally favor tax cuts, and therefore speedy consideration would not appear unusual. While

TABLE 8. COMPLETION OF MAJOR INITIATIVES (FIRST YEAR)

Transition	Tax Cut		All Major Initiatives Completed		
	Day completed	Bush improved	Day completed	Number of initiatives	Completion rate
G. W. Bush	107	22%	218	5	40%
Previous	137		133	12	62%
Clinton	n/a		142	7	57%
GHW Bush	n/a		205	7	43%
Reagan	167		145	7	100%
Carter	105		94	17	53%
Nixon	105		116	9	44%
Kennedy	n/a		98	25	72%
Regime type					
Unified	139	21%	111	12	61%
Divided	136	24%	155	8	62%

Source: Compiled by Terry Sullivan from *The Congressional Record, Public Papers of the President,* and *Weekly Compilation of Presidential Documents.*

this criticism seems reasonable, the data do not support its premise. The record of other administrations proposing tax cuts makes clear that these policies do not always carry immediate and overwhelming support. By comparison with previous transitions, for example, the Congress completed work on the Bush tax cut a month sooner than the average (an improvement efficiency rating of 22 percent), including a month improvement over the typical unified government. Of particular note, the Bush tax cut moved through Congress a whopping sixty days faster than the previous supply-side tax cut during the Reagan administration.

That experience with planning did not, however, carry over to the administration's other policy initiatives. For example, consider initiatives completed by Congress during the first year of administrations. Here, the George W. Bush record, at 40 percent, represents the least responsive completion rate among the previous transitions. President Carter's experience, often cited as the exemplar of poor agenda formation, for example, scored thirteen percentage points higher than did the 2001 transition. Presidents Reagan and Kennedy hold the records for divided and unified completion rates, respectively. Given the numbers of initiatives set out in congressional messages (see table 7), the 2001 transition record does not illustrate the virtues of a focused agenda, even though they quite clearly employed one.[53]

Summary

Much of their experience with long-term planning seems to have benefited the 2001 transition. The Bush transition moved through the presentation of their agenda faster than any previous transition. And they made remarkable progress in ushering their highest priority initiative, their tax cut, through the Congressional process. But the overall agenda did not fare well. Some of that lackluster performance can be traced to the transfer of the majority leadership from the president's party in the summer of 2001 as well as the 9/11 crisis, both likely to have abnormally lengthened their record of completion.

THE MEASURE OF TRANSITIONS

The Baker Institute Forum on the White House Chief of Staff set as a goal to bring public attention to the proper conduct of a presidential transition. Each participating former chief of staff lent his advice and prestige without regard to partisan sensibilities. They had no idea who would win the 2000 presidential election. Nor did they consider the possibility that one of their number would eventually become vice president of the United States or that someone closely associated with so many of them would soon join their select group. Instead, they participated as an act of public service, hoping to shape planning for and management in the institution that each held in such high regard.

Based on the advice of the Forum and the standards used here, the George W. Bush transition established an exemplar. In discipline, balance, focus, and planning, the Bush White House guided itself through a tumultuous beginning to make a well-orchestrated start. As the comparative data suggests, their achievement constitutes an historic accomplishment.

Of course, every presidential transition does not set out to achieve academic goals, any more than they set out to stumble their way through the first hundred days. That so many have experienced such distress stands as testament to the inherent difficulty of these simultaneously political and civic acts. Managing to govern from the White House, from within the nerve center, has no parallel. No national presidential campaign, no governorship, no global corporation, no other elected Washington position presents its occupants or their staffs with equivalent challenges. For this reason, former presidents become trusted confidants of the incumbent, regardless of their partisan differences, and those who have occupied the management responsibilities for those presidents have become the best available advisors for those who enter the nerve center each day.

TABLE 9. COMPARISONS BETWEEN INFORMATION SOURCES

Data source	Meetings with			Press Conferences	Television or other media	Travel		Time off
	Congress	Cabinet	Interests			Foreign	Domestic	
Kennedy Estimated (S/G)[a]	3/3	2/2	4/4	10/10	7/7	0/0	1/2	0/2
Actual[b]	50	5	28	10	6	0	2	11
Carter Estimated (S/G)	26/7	15/15	37/12	6/6	3/4	0/0	3/4	7/4
Actual	74	15	69	6	8	0	3	9

[a]S = data compiled by Terry Sullivan from *Congressional Record*, *Public Papers of the President*, and *Weekly Compilation of Presidential Documents*.
G = data compiled by Terry Sullivan from Gergen's tables.
[b]Actual figures compiled by Terry Sullivan from National Archives, "Presidential Appointments Logs," John F. Kennedy Presidential Library and Jimmy Carter Presidential Library.

The transition process needs still more attention. The Bush transition team achieved a great deal based on their advance preparations, but the planning apparatus could be further improved. The public deserves better, especially when they can easily get better. Two examples taken from the hallmark accomplishments of the Bush transition illustrate the need for a stronger transition effort.

Targeting Personnel

Setting and meeting personnel goals constitutes one of the highest accomplishments of the Bush transition. That success rested on two elements. First, the planners committed their early efforts to identifying positions, not nominees. And they focused on identifying positions that set policy. To identify positions, they relied on the *Plum Book,* a joint effort of the Congress and Office of Personnel Management listing "currently" noncompetitive positions. Unfortunately, these two agencies do not release their listing until after the election. That schedule reflects the troublesome assumption that the president-elect's team does not need to know about the government's personnel structure until after the election. The *Plum Book* released at election time in 2000 carried 8,129 titles. No one can master the shape of these positions in the critical, and short, period of time after the election. The government should complete the *Plum Book* well before the election, presumably during June or July of the election year.[54] Otherwise, the transition planners must rely on the previous publication developed four years earlier. Since many of the policy-making positions will have changed during those four years, reflecting statutory and reorganization changes, the transition planners have a far more difficult task than necessary identifying key personnel.

Given that fact, two recommendations seems worthwhile:

    1. The congressional leadership and the president should make certain that they set new policy on the scheduled release of the *Plum Book* by moving forward its public release to June.

    2. The congressional leadership and the president should make certain that the new compilation identifies the critical policy-making positions in the government.

Planning for Discretion

While clearly an effective tool for planning, discovering the outlines of presidential activities should not constitute such a mystery. Both of the most successful transitions of the past six decades have devoted a good deal of effort (as suggested by the details in table 7) at assaying what a president must do on a routine basis and what discretion a president might have available. They have made valiant efforts to project an idea of the possible and these ideas have guided their advance preparations. Unfortunately, they have based their judgments on the most rudimentary information. Meanwhile, the National Archives and its partners in the Secret Service, the presidential appointments office, and the White House ushers maintain the best information for such planning: a minute-by-minute log of the president's activities. They have done so since Dwight Eisenhower's administration. And while this information could provide invaluable insights into these two critical questions (responsibilities and discretion), transition planners have not had access to it.

Table 9 reports a comparison between those public data sources used by the planners reported earlier in table 7 and the actual figures derived from two recently available presidential appointments logs, one made available by the John Kennedy Library and one made available by the Jimmy Carter Library. The table shows that in some areas, the public data usually employed by planners produces satisfactory estimates of activities. These include those activities that the National Archives itself makes a special effort to enumerate (such as presidential news conferences) and those that generate a certain amount of press coverage (such as presidential foreign travel).[55] Note, though, that among the three measures used in the travel category, estimating the amount of time the president takes off appears a difficult task without the use of the appointments logs. For Kennedy, the Gergen and Rove studies missed the mark considerably. For Carter, the best estimate, using the *Presidential Papers* series and cross-checking it with Lexis/Nexis, still missed the president's down time by a factor of almost 30 percent.

Modern methods of newsgathering have improved greatly their coverage of the president's cabinet meetings. While they missed a considerable percentage of Kennedy's, they reported accurately the number of Carter cabinet meetings. Normally public sources did a miserable job, however, of estimating the number of meetings the president took. The table reports two key types, those with congressional leaders and those with interest groups, both representative of central presidential responsibilities in policy making. The numbers for congressional contacts seem particularly troublesome given the likely conclusions planners might draw about how much time the president normally invests in legislative activities. Here the number cited for actual contacts only notes contacts with congressional leaders (partisan and committee leaders) and only those in which the president's meeting took at least six minutes. Given the value of the president's time, the latter standard excludes a substantial number of encounters with the congressional leadership in which the president *briefly* makes a specific request or obtains a specific piece of information or settles a specific strategic issue. Thus, even the numbers reported here present a conservative view of how much time a president typically invests in each of these activities.

These very conservative estimates of actual time suggest that planners have developed a disastrously low approximation of presidential activity. For example, the estimates for Kennedy interactions with congressional leaders missed the actual figures by a factor of 1,567 percent. Quite obviously, the public reports on Kennedy do a miserable job of capturing his involvement with legislative affairs. But even for Jimmy Carter, typically thought to have paid little attention to congressional politics, the estimates underrepresented his involvement by around 200 percent.[56] Given the fact that Carter had a daily morning briefing on congressional relations, which other presidents have not had, and which did not normally get noted in public accounts of the president's schedule, these underestimates perpetuate misleading public images of Carter's legislative activity. And that image of the presidency, as less engaged in legislative affairs, does a disservice to those who want to know the "normal" demands on a president's time. Indeed, it reinforces further the belief that properly appreciating scale in the nerve center represents the single most important issue for transition planners. Even the most conscientious and motivated researchers will miss the actual record by a very large amount.

Similarly, though less inaccurate than for legislative affairs, the data on interest group contact probably would give planners a better picture of these activities as well. For both presidents covered in these comparisons, the amount of error ranges from about 700 percent for Kennedy and 200 percent for Carter. The estimates did manage to approximate the relative proportions of meetings correctly: more legislative meetings than interest group meetings. Since these differences probably reflect the fact that responsibilities and duties squeeze the amount of time left for coalition maintenance, some useful information about demands gets conveyed even though the studies miss the details.

The details, though, often tell the most important stories. For example, the differences in legislative and interest group contact probably suggest that these responsibilities would then fall mostly to the White House staff under its chief, thus emphasizing more the role of the president's staff. Or these data may suggest that interest groups simply get ignored more than we imagine, implying in turn that their causes get conveyed more through the media than through personal contact with the White House. In any case, the general view of the president as more engaged with interests appears a highly misleading exaggeration.

And these data do not begin to address the questions raised earlier about administrative, diplomatic, and partisan responsibilities. We simply have no estimate of how much of the president's time these responsibilities consume, and without them, we cannot (nor can any planner) estimate properly how to preserve the president's discretionary commitments.

No one has an interest, partisan or otherwise, in keeping this useful information from a potential new president's team. To the contrary, everyone has a common interest in making it easier to understand the challenges any new team will face. Proper transition planning should move beyond the current practice of "guesstimating," using what now appears to be sadly inadequate public data. Instead, transition planners should be able to incorporate more accurate and thereby more suggestive data.

As such, it seems reasonable to add the following recommendation to the previous two:

> 3. The president should instruct the archivist of the United States to collaborate with outside experts in preparing a detailed and scientific analysis of past presidents' schedules during their transition periods from inauguration through the first 180 days.

Though White Houses work for policy goals and not academic ones, the civic milestones set out here represent objective standards with which to assess governing. The information requirements proposed here represent objective needs with which to support governing. Both also represent solid advice from those who have borne the burdens. To the extent that all Americans, partisans and academics, have a stake in a successful transfer of power and responsibility, these standards deserve further attention. When the government has met these objectives and provided this information, the advice of the former chiefs of staff will have fully reached those who enter the nerve center. And as they eloquently demonstrated by their collective voice, that constitutes a service to us all.

Notes
1. Card did not know about his selection as chief of staff until after breakfast with Governor Bush on November 2. The candidate and his transition planners thought they had offered Card the job a week earlier. Calling him at his Virginia home on October 28, 2000, Governor Bush had told Card to get ready to take on the "big one." The governor had also used this language before the Republican convention, when he had told Card to "keep his dance card open for the 'big one.'" Convinced that Governor Bush had asked him to direct the transition, after the October 28 phone call, Card left for a two-day briefing with Clay Johnson in Austin and with former President Bush in Houston before flying on to meet

with the governor on the campaign trail in Florida. Not until the end of Thursday's breakfast did Card conclude that the governor had actually asked him to consider serving as the White House chief of staff. For his part, Clay Johnson had simply assumed that Card understood what the governor intended and had never broached the subject specifically during their briefing. "Interview with Andrew H. Card, Jr.," James A. Baker III Institute White House Transition Project, Terry Sullivan, Dec. 7, 2001, Washington, D.C.

2. These included the three "chiefs" of the troika (Baker, Meese, and Deaver), James Baker alone, Donald Regan, Howard Baker, Jr., Kenneth Duberstein, and then John Sununu. "Interview of Andrew H. Card, Jr.," James A. Baker III Institute White House Transition Project, Terry Sullivan, Apr. 10, 2002, the White House, Washington, D.C.

3. One might argue that Card had an additional advantage in that the president-elect had designated as transition leader (what Card had thought of as the "big one") another well-seasoned White House veteran and former White House chief of staff (and Forum participant) Richard Cheney. Clay Johnson had convinced Governor Bush that the transition would need a unified head and that Cheney should lead the effort (see Clay Johnson III, "The 2000–2001 Presidential Transition—Planning, Goals and Reality," in *The White House World: Transitions, Organizations, and Office Operations,* ed. Martha J. Kumar and Terry Sullivan (College Station: Texas A&M University Press, 2003). Their plan called for the Cheney-Johnson team to focus on developing the executive branch transitions, leaving Card with the full responsibility for the White House. That division matched arrangements in the George H. W. Bush transition (see "Interview with Andrew Card," White House 2001 Project, White House Interview Program, Martha J. Kumar, May 25, 1999, Cambridge, Mass.).

4. "Interview with Clay Johnson," James A. Baker III Institute White House Transition Project, Terry Sullivan, Sept. 26, 2002, Washington, D.C.

5. For example, the Baker Institute's Presidential Transition Project, the White House 2001 Project, and the Brookings Institution's Presidential Appointee Initiative, among other scholarly efforts, contributed to Clay Johnson's planning effort as they also did to efforts taking place at the Al Gore for President campaign.

6. For example, most of the transition planners (like Roy Neel) had substantial experience with the Clinton operation, especially under Leon Panetta, Erskine Bowles, and John Podesta.

7. Johnson, "The 2000–2001 Presidential Transition."

8. By the time the governor had asked Card to serve as chief of staff, the transition planning team had not circulated these goals. Card, in fact, had not seen them until a year later. "Interview with Andrew H. Card, Jr.," James A. Baker III Institute White House Transition Project, Terry Sullivan, Apr. 10, 2002, the White House, Washington, D.C.

9. Besides the White House 2001 Project, these other institutions included the Brookings Institution, the James A. Baker III Institute, American Enterprise Institute, Kennedy School of Government, Burns Academy of Leadership, Cato Institute, Heritage Foundation, and Center for the Study of the Presidency.

10. Martha J. Kumar, George C. Edwards III, James Pfiffner, and Terry Sullivan, "Meeting the Freight Train Head On: Planning for the Transition to Power," in

The White House World. See also Alvin S. Felzenberg, ed., *The Keys to a Successful Presidency* (Washington, D.C.: Heritage Foundation, 2000), especially chapter 1. See also Charles O. Jones, *Passages to the Presidency: From Campaigning to Governing* (Washington, D.C.: Brookings Institution, 1999).

11. "Interview with Richard Cheney," White House 2001 Project, White House Interview Program, Martha J. Kumar, July 29, 1999, Dallas, Tex.

12. Similar points about managing the president's time to avoid poor decisions also found in Jones, *Passages to the Presidency*.

13. "Interview with Richard Cheney," White House 2001 Project, White House Interview Program, Martha J. Kumar, July 29, 1999, Dallas, Tex.

14. "Interview with Pendleton James," White House 2001 Project, White House Interview Program, Martha J. Kumar, Nov. 8, 1999, Washington, D.C.

15. "Interview with Constance Horner," White House 2001 Project, White House Interview Program, Martha J. Kumar, Mar. 23, 1999, Washington D.C.

16. Chase Untermeyer, quoted in Felzenberg, *Keys to a Successful Presidency*.

17. "Interview with Clay Johnson," James A. Baker III Institute White House Transition Project, Terry Sullivan, Sept. 26, 2002, Washington, D.C.

18. As Bradley Patterson points out, all of the White House staff serve at the president's pleasure. Hence, the White House has no professional staff. Only tradition identifies these staff as separated from the president's completely political appointments.

19. "Interview with Andrew Card," White House 2001 Project, White House Interview Program, Martha J. Kumar, May 25, 1999, Cambridge, Mass.

20. "Interview with James A. Baker III," White House 2001 Project, White House Interview Program, Martha J. Kumar and Terry Sullivan, Nov. 16, 1999, Houston, Tex.

21. "Interview with David Gergen," White House 2001 Project, White House Interview Program, Martha Kumar, June 24, 1997, Washington, D.C.

22. "Interview with James Cicconi, Philip Brady, and Andrew Card," Martha J. Kumar, Sept. 19, 1997, Washington, D.C., quoted in Martha J. Kumar, "Feasibility Study for the Pew Charitable Trusts."

23. Gergen's study covered the daily activities of the previous five transitions: Roosevelt, Eisenhower, Kennedy, Nixon, and Carter. Each study produced a calendar of actions and activities for the first one hundred days of each administration. Gergen then compiled these data into a general memo on five areas of activities. David Gergen, "Study on Presidential Activities," Papers of James A. Baker III, Rice University Archives.

24. Table 10 disaggregates the six categories in the Gergen study into specific measures. Note, though, that "convening Congress" occurred only once (FDR).

25. "Interview with Thomas F. McLarty," White House 2001 Project, White House Interview Program, Martha J. Kumar, Nov. 16, 1999, Washington, D.C.

26. "Interview with Andrew H. Card, Jr.," White House 2001 Project, White House Interview Program, Martha Kumar, May 25, 1999, Cambridge, Mass

27. "Interview with James A. Baker III," White House 2001 Project, Martha Kumar and Terry Sullivan, Nov. 16, 1999, Houston, Tex.

28. In a common campaign experience among Democrats, the candidate assigns relatively junior staff to transition planning only to have senior advisors jettison those plans after the election. To avoid that common experience, the White House

TABLE 10. DISAGGREGATED MEASURES USED IN GERGEN CATEGORIES

Constitutional	Foreign Affairs	Domestic Affairs	Domestic Appearances	Press and Media Appearances	Miscellaneous
Commander in chief	Diplomatic visits	Cabinet	Travel	First press conference	Gestures
Reprieves granted	Missions sent	Congressional	Vacations	Press conferences	Scandals
State of Union	Travel	Supreme Court	Speeches	Media speeches	
Convene Congress		Governors			
Treaties signed		Mayors			
		Political party			
		Agencies			
		Special interests			
		Former presidents			

2001 Project and the Baker Institute's Transition Project recommended directly attaching the transition planning function to the campaign's highest leadership.

29. See Martha J. Kumar, "Recruiting and Organizing the White House Staff," in *The White House World*.

30. "Interview with Clay Johnson," James A. Baker III Institute White House Transition Project, Terry Sullivan, Sept. 26, 2002, Washington, D.C.

31. The analysis relies on the standard measure of efficiency: the "lambda" statistic.

32. The administration asked twenty-one inspectors general to remain, six of the senior leadership at the Central Intelligence Agency, and ten of the leadership at State.

33. This document, a joint publication of the Congress and the Office of Personnel Management, lists noncompetitive government positions. The analysis relies on the 1996 *Plum Book* because the Bush transition planners did not receive the

2000 versions until after the election. The 1996 *Plum Book* describes some 8,125 positions in the executive branch subject in some circumstances to "noncompetitive" appointment.

34. Excluding cabinet secretaries and EX-I personnel already covered pares the number to 122.

35. See Martha J. Kumar, "Establishing a White House Staff and Its Operations," in *The White House World*. Clay Johnson recalled that George Shultz had encouraged them to establish such a connection between the White House and the cabinet. "Interview with Clay Johnson," James A. Baker III Institute, White House Transition Project, Terry Sullivan, Sept. 26, 2002, Washington, D.C.

36. In most cabinet departments the press secretary does not occupy a PAS position. Hence, the PAI database did not track them. Where the cabinet department had an assistant secretary for public affairs, the data included that position.

37. Kumar, "Establishing a White House Staff and Its Operations."

38. "Interview with Roy Neel," White House 2001 Project, White House Interview Program, Martha J. Kumar, June 15, 1999, Washington, D.C.

39. "Interview with Clay Johnson," James A. Baker III Institute White House Transition Project, Terry Sullivan, Sept. 26, 2002, Washington, D.C. "Interview with Andrew H. Card, Jr.," James A. Baker III Institute, White House Transition Project, Terry Sullivan, Apr. 10, 2002, the White House, Washington, D.C.

40. Richard Brookhiser, "The Mind of George W. Bush," *Atlantic Monthly,* Apr., 2003, pp. 55–69.

41. "Interview with Andrew H. Card, Jr.," James A. Baker III Institute, White House Transition Project, Terry Sullivan, Apr. 10, 2002, the White House, Washington, D.C.

42. Ibid.

43. "Interview with John Podesta," James A. Baker III Institute White House Transition Project, Terry Sullivan, Sept. 26, 2001, Washington, D.C.

44. "Interview with Andrew H. Card, Jr.," James A. Baker III Institute, White House Transition Project, Terry Sullivan, Apr. 10, 2002, the White House, Washington, D.C.

45. The two programs overlapped in the Kennedy, Nixon, and Carter transitions, with Gergen covering Truman and Roosevelt and Rove covering Reagan, George H. W. Bush, and Clinton.

46. Gergen's study covered twenty-five activities in six groups (see note 24). Rove's list included: foreign/domestic travel, days off, major initiatives, executive orders, messages to Congress, national TV appearances, news conferences, joint session speeches, and congressional, NGO, or cabinet meetings. "Interview with Karl Rove," James A. Baker III Institute, White House Transition Project, Terry Sullivan, Dec. 12, 2002, Washington, D.C.

47. Ibid.

48. See Bennett Roth and Karen Masterson, "Coalition Unveils Managed-care Bill, Bush Aide Looks to Derail Measure," *Houston Chronicle,* Feb. 7, 2001, p. A1.

49. See Dan Morgan, "Business Backs Bush Tax Cut; Under Pressure, Groups Agree to Defer Push for Wider Relief," *Washington Post,* Mar. 4, 2001, p. A1.

50. See Mile Allen and Allen Sipress, "Attacks Refocus on How to Fight Terrorism," *Washington Post,* Sept. 26, 2001, p. A3, and David Balz, "Bush's Political Guru Finds Himself on Periphery," *Washington Post,* Oct. 31, 2001, p. A3.

51. Though Karl Rove clearly winces at the term's use, others in the White House refer openly to the silly title. An additional group—Card designated it the "Karen and Karl" meeting, created in the operational shake-up following 9/11—brought Card and the other two senior counselors together with the president for what Card described as "midrange" planning. The involvement of the president in this kind of group seems like a hallmark of the Bush management style.

52. See Dona Milbank, "Serious 'Strategery'; As Rove Launches Elaborate Political Effort, Some See a Nascent Clintonian 'War Room,'" *Washington Post*, Apr. 22, 2001, p. A1.

53. In addition, recall that the Bush administration mishandled a number of regulatory matters during their initial transition period, including a recurring bout with regulations on arsenic in urban water supplies. These stumbles, however, originated in the Clinton administration, apparently as ongoing issues that they had held in reserve presuming that a newly elected Al Gore would prefer to settle them on his own terms. The election outcome short-circuited those plans and left the regulations for the Bush administration to discover them as pending.

54. Some legislative proposals have set the time for release of the *Plum Book* at the close of the national party conventions. While an improvement on the current timing, the proposed release could come earlier without harm. The government need only make the document available and allow the candidate's planners to work from it whenever they plan to, even if that schedule begins long before their party's convention. Often by June the parties through their primaries have already selected their presumptive candidates and transition planning has begun in earnest, as happened with the Bush for President planners.

55. See Martha J. Kumar, "'Does This Constitute a Press Conference?' Defining and Measuring Modern Presidential Press Conferences," *Presidential Studies Quarterly* 33, no. 1 (Mar., 2003).

56. See Thomas P. O'Neill, *Man of the House* (New York: Random House, 1987).

Sponsors' Acknowledgments

The James A. Baker III Institute for Public Policy of Rice University is pleased to have presented this forum on the role of the White House chief of staff. It was the very first program that the Baker Institute hosted in Washington, D.C. Since then, the Institute has hosted similar forums on the national security advisor and the secretary of the treasury. In each of these forums, as with the chief of staff, our goal was to bring together former office holders to talk about the challenges of the job they had held in order to further the proper administration of government. This forum of the former White House chiefs of staff is unique in that we have secured participation from almost all of those who have held the job in the modern White House, which we date from President Richard Nixon's administration onward. Their participation in the record of this forum has created the only complete record of the former chiefs. The Forum has created a record on the office and its place in governing to serve those scholars and journalists who describe administrations' histories as well as shape public understanding of the White House. We also wanted to assist new presidents and their teams as they prepare to take office to understand the central functions of this critical office.

While the Baker Institute's forum was an important gathering in its own right, it was also part of a broad, philanthropic, nonpartisan effort to smooth the way for the new administration that took office in January, 2001. Other institutions who participated with the Baker Institute in preparing the transition were in the audience for the Forum and they included the Brookings Institution, the American Enterprise Institute, and the Heritage Foundation. In particular, the Institute cooperated closely with the White House 2001 Project's White House Interview Program directed by Professor Martha Joynt Kumar.

With this forum on the White House chief of staff, the Baker Institute initiated a growing partnership with the Woodrow Wilson International Center for Scholars of the Smithsonian Institution. For years, I worked closely with the Wilson Center's director, the Honorable Lee Hamilton, when he served as the distinguished chair of the House Committee on Foreign Relations and I served as assistant secretary of state and then U.S. ambassador to Syria and then Israel. Under his leadership, Lee has given the Center a new lease on life and a new direction that the Baker Institute is proud to be a part of. The Wilson Center's staff gave us an expert foothold in Washington and facilitated every aspect of the Forum.

Also, I want to acknowledge the efforts of the Baker Institute's own staff. Putting on such an event flawlessly, from fifteen hundred miles away, requires unparalleled professionalism. As an example of how every detail was anticipated by our staff, one of the former chiefs had delayed a previous appointment so he could attend the Forum. When he did leave, holding off until the last possible minute, he was concerned he would not be able to negotiate the complex hallways of the Reagan Office Building and its equally arcane parking garage. Suddenly one of our staff, Mr. Jay Guerrero, appeared at his side to escort him to his car. The day before, Jay and the Institute's associate director, W. O. King, had personally walked every one of the Reagan Building hallways and through the garage in order to be sure they could escort any of the former chiefs of staff who might need a hand. The same thing happened when the FBI appeared in the middle of the Forum to escort two of our participants to an emergency security briefing for a national commission in which they participated. The Institute's staff did not miss a beat. They were professional, foresighted, and prepared.

The Forum covered four topics. The first three assessed the White House through the administration's tenure, running from the White House transition, through reorganizing and refocusing the president's team, to the reelection drive and eventually closing out of an administration. As a professional in the White House and the executive branch for thirty years, I have seen the importance of each of these times for an administration. I know those panels captured a great deal of what is important to governing from the White House. The last panel directly addressed the role of the White House chief of staff within the larger governing community, working with Congress and the executive branch, with interest groups and with the press.

Of course, the Forum would not have addressed a single one of these topics, would not have influenced the public's understanding of early transition planning, and would not have had such an impact on the White House transition in 2001 or on future transitions had it not been for the foresight and leadership of James A. Baker III, the Institute's honorary chairman. Having seen governing from a number of important vantage points—campaigning, cabinet, chief of staff—his guidance became the foundation for this forum.

The Baker Institute had an extraordinary opportunity with this Washington forum to garner the collective wisdom of these few people who have served our nation with distinction. Now, with this book, we have another opportunity to preserve that record of wisdom for those who follow; to make their jobs a little easier, and, through that, make America's business run more smoothly for the good of us all.

—Edward P. Djerejian, Director
James A. Baker III Institute for Public Policy

I want to thank Ed Djerejian and Terry Sullivan of the James A. Baker III Institute for Public Policy of Rice University. This forum was the first of a series of meetings coordinated between our two institutions. It was a pleasure for those of us at the Wilson Center to work with the Baker Institute to put on this remarkable program.

The Wilson Center is the nation's living memorial to the twenty-eighth president. Woodrow Wilson was the only president of the United States who held a Ph.D. He was a scholar and a practitioner. He felt passionately that people engaged in public policy and people of ideas were engaged, as he put it, "in a common enterprise." Both the Baker Institute and the Wilson Center work to bridge the gap between the theory and the practice of public policy by bringing together the thinkers and the doers, the scholars and the policy makers, in the confident hope that from their dialogue better public policy will emerge. The Forum on the White House Chief of Staff represents just such a bridge and I am glad to see that its efforts have played such an important role in smoothing the way for a new president's team.

—Lee H. Hamilton, Director
Woodrow Wilson International Center for Scholars

Index

Untermeyer, Chase, 130, 131

vetting: of appointees, 42; of information, 74
vice-president, 24, 30, 55, 65, 81, 89, 100, 102, 110

Watson, Jack H., Jr.: biography, 21
White House decision-making: affecting policy, 57, 133; agenda formation, 65; agreements with President, 29, 51; balance in, 62; controlling access to President, 29, 38, 51, 54, 55, 56, 64, 67; controlling the process, xiv, xvi, xvii, 30, 39, 51, 55, 57, 60, 67, 102, 115, 116, 117, 124; crisis, 70; discipline, 144, 145, 146, 147; effectiveness, xvi; focus in, 133, 134; orchestration, 64; politics affecting, 25; president, relationship with Chief of Staff, xv, 29, 38, 43, 44, 52, 64, 103, 110; responsibilities/skills necessary for success, xvii, 34, 62, 65, 67, 68, 91, 123; rhythm of tenure, 10–11; role, Chief of Staff, 24, 26, 37, 58, 109, 112, 115, 124, 167; speeches affecting, 117; staff position, xiii, xv, 28, 99; structuring process, xv; uniqueness of Chief of Staff, 102, 103
White House learning: campaign experience, xvii, 24, 27, 31, 32, 36, 59, 99, 143; preparations, xv, 98; preparations, 5, 6; surprises, 114; Washington experience, 64, 99
White House Office: staffing, 131

White House operations: and 9/11, 166; chain of command, 56; different from business, 53; discipline, 8, 130, 131; effectiveness, 9, 133; for transition 2001, 130–36; pace, 70; partisanship, 5, 7; rhythm of tenure, 7, 10; scale, 5; scale in transition 2001, 130–31, 137–38; scrutiny, 5, 6; two dilemmas, 4, 7, 8, 7–10
White House organization, 27, 30, 33, 38, 49, 50, 53, 58, 74, 89, 94, 103; Brownlow Committee, 13; different from others, 5; models of, 25, 45
White House staff: balance for transition 2001, 132; balance in trasition 2001, 142–43; firing, 29, 44, 53, 58, 105; importance of, 4, 33, 41, 42, 68, 70, 123, 132–33; necessity of, 50; numbers, 58, 59, 74
White House staffing: changes in, 51; in transition 2001, 138, 139
White House Transition Project: White House 2001 program, 128, 162
White House work: balance in, 32, 49, 61, 62; disruption of, 53; division of labor, 28; for transition 2001, 130–36; four P's, xiv; length of day, 41; partisanship as challenge, 7; rhythm of tenure, 10–11; scale as challenge, 5–6; scale in transition 2001, 130–31, 137–38; scrutiny as challenge, 6
Wirthlin, Richard, 45; transition planning, 134

Zelleck, Robert, 42